FOCUSED DISCIPLINE

THE QUIET STRENGTH BEHIND EVERY GREAT ACHIEVEMENT

HARRIS D. McFARLARE

FOCUSED DISCIPLINE

Copyright ©2025 by Harris D. Mcfarlare

Hardcover ISBN: 978-1-965593-63-9
Paperback ISBN: 978-1-965593-64-6

All rights reserved. No part of this publication may be reproduced, distributed, or transmitted in any form or by any means, including photocopying, recording, or other electronic or mechanical methods without the prior written permission of the author except in the case of brief quotations embodied in reviews and certain other non-commercial uses permitted by copyright law.

Published by Cornerstone Publishing

A Division of Cornerstone Creativity Group LLC
Info@thecornerstonepublishers.com
www.thecornerstonepublishers.com

Author's Contact

To book the author to speak at your next event or to order bulk copies of this book, please, use the information below:

info@dimensionministries.org

Printed in the United States of America.

DEDICATION

To my wife-Jennifer!

Your life is a living example of disciplined grace. You've shown me that discipline is not control, but love in action. Thank you for inspiring me every day to do the work, to stay the course, and to lead with purpose.

To my daughter, Nicole!

May you always chase the stars,

write your own story,

and know that I believe in you .

In memory of my beloved mother and father, who instilled in me the seeds of discipline , perseverance, and reverence for God. Your sacrifices were my first lessons in discipline. This book is a testament to your quiet strength and enduring love.

CONTENTS

DEDICATION iii

INTRODUCTION vii

1. Why Focused Discipline? 1
2. The Power of a Clear Goal 11
3. Time is Life 23
4. Self-Image and Personal Success 37
5. Know Your Why 51
6. Desire, Determination, and Discipline 61
7. The Discipline of Focus 73
8. The Habit of Showing Up 87
9. The Power of Follow-Through 99
10. The Power of Saying No 115
11. Resilience: Staying Strong When Life Hits Hard ... 129
12. Attitude is Everything 149

13. Marriage and Mission; Partnering for Purpose 163

14. Objection Doesn't Mean Rejection 173

15. Rooted in God - Prayer, Promises, and Power 185

CONCLUSION 195

INTRODUCTION

THE CALL TO FOCUSED DISCIPLINE

Every generation searches for the secret behind extraordinary lives. We admire greatness, applaud achievement, and celebrate visible results. Whether in business, leadership, ministry, or personal growth, a quieter force lies beneath the surface. It isn't glamorous. It doesn't trend on social media. Yet it is the difference between those who drift aimlessly and those who decide with intention. That force is *Focused Discipline*.

This truth has defined my life. I was born in Jamaica to hardworking parents who taught me the values of faith, perseverance, hard work, and sacrifice. I arrived in the United States with nothing but a Diploma in Management from the Institute of Management and Production, which is now The University of the Commonwealth Caribbean, a suitcase, and a dream—no roadmap, no guarantees, just a burning desire to make something of my life. That suitcase held a few clothes and maybe a keepsake or two; however, it was my heart that carried the real weight: the hope of a future I hadn't yet seen and the determination to make something of my life.

I learned that life may not always be fair; it rewards those who are faithful, focused, disciplined, and unwilling to fold under pressure. I didn't have connections; I had conviction. I didn't have resources; I had resilience.

I started at the bottom, sorting mail in the mailroom of a major company. I didn't stay there long. Within a few months, I was promoted to an analyst position that started an onward and upward trajectory of mental muscle, keeping me going through every storm and setback.

I worked long hours, often taking on two or three jobs to get by. Late nights and early mornings became routine to keep my dream alive. Then I entered the world of sales on a part-time basis, without any formal training; I learned quickly. Every rejection was a classroom. Every *no* built a little more grit in me. Over time, I began to recognize a pattern. It wasn't the smartest person in the room who advanced: it was the one who showed up. It was the one who kept showing up. It was the one who worked hard at improving their skill level. It was the one who stayed when others quit. That was when I realized that talent may open the door, but discipline is what keeps it open.

It wasn't always easy. Days of doubt, moments of temptation to quit, and challenges seemed bigger than my resources and mental capacity. In those moments, I leaned on my faith and remembered the words of my mother, who often reminded me, "If you put God first and stay the course, nothing will be impossible." Her wisdom, deep faith, trust, and confidence in God carried me through setbacks and propelled me into opportunities I could never have imagined had it not been for my absolute faith.

The very discipline that elevated me from the mailroom became the compass that guided me in building businesses, starting a ministry, and nurturing both past and emerging leaders. Through each chapter, I came to understand that discipline is not defined by innate talent or perfect knowledge—it is the quiet strength of showing up consistently with unwavering focus, bold courage, and steadfast faith.

This book is not about chasing quick wins or momentary bursts of inspiration. It is about building a life that stands the test of time. A life where clarity guides your steps, commitment fuels your consistency, and purpose anchors your progress. Focused Discipline is not about perfection; it's about persistence. It's the bridge between who you are now and who you are becoming.

As you turn these pages, you'll discover how to align your discipline with your God-given purpose, how to set clear goals, how to master your time, and how to cultivate the inner image that sustains outer success. You'll also see how prayer, faith, and daily practices create momentum that no setback can silence.

If you're in sales, marketing, business, ministry, or leadership, wanting to advance in your job, improve your grades, or simply trying to launch something new, this book is written for you. You may wonder how to keep going when your motivation is gone. You may have started strong, yet feel like your momentum is slipping. Or maybe you're just trying to figure out how to start something. You are not alone. I've been there. I've wrestled with those same questions. Throughout this book, I want to offer you more than advice. I want to provide you with language for what you're feeling, tools for what you're facing, and stories to remind you that a breakthrough is possible.

I invite you to lean in—not just with your mind, but with your heart. Let these words remind you that your destiny is not shaped by chance but forged by choice. The choice before you is clear: Distraction or discipline? Convenience or commitment? Drifting or deciding?

May this book serve as both a compass and a companion on your journey. May you discover, as I have, that when you choose *Focused Discipline*, you are not just building habits; you are building a life that honors God, impacts others, and leaves a legacy that will outlive you.

—Rev. Harris D. McFarlane

CHAPTER 1

WHY FOCUSED DISCIPLINE?

"No discipline seems pleasant at the time, but painful. Later on, however, it produces a harvest of righteousness and peace for those who have been trained by it."
— HEBREWS 12:11 (NIV)

There are two kinds of people in the world: those who drift and those who decide. The drifters allow life to push them wherever the tides take them. The decision-makers, however, are grounded. They know where they are, they know where they are going, and they move in that direction with quiet intensity. At the center of that strength is what I call Focused Discipline. It isn't flashy. It doesn't get trending hash tags. But it changes everything. It's what turns dreams into plans and plans into action. It's what keeps a person committed when the applause stops, when the crowd moves on, and when the feelings of motivation have faded. Focused Discipline isn't based on emotion; it's anchored in clarity, commitment, and consistency. It's not about how you feel today; it's about what you've decided about your tomorrow.

When I first arrived in the United States, I didn't have a glamorous start. I wasn't handed a golden opportunity. What I had was a clear vision and a commitment to make it work. My entry point into the corporate world was the mailroom. I didn't despise it; I saw it as an open door—the beginning of something greater. I treated it as such. Within three months, I moved from the mailroom to an analyst position at a major corporation. That wasn't luck. That wasn't magic. That was Focused Discipline in action. I delivered mail with purpose. I made connections. I stayed alert to opportunities. I didn't allow where I was to define who I was or where I could go.

THE CORE OF FOCUSED DISCIPLINE

Focused Discipline is not just about working hard; it is about working with direction. It's waking up every morning with clarity on your mission, even when progress feels slow. It's about the deliberate and intentional choice to pursue goals that matter—goals that align with your values and your purpose. You see, hustle without purpose will wear you out. You can be busy and still be going nowhere. But when your effort aligns with a clear goal and a committed heart, that's when momentum begins to build. That's where power is found.

Focused Discipline begins with knowing where you are. This might sound simple, yet many people ignore this step. They avoid the hard truths of their current situation. They pretend they're further along than they are. You can't change what you don't acknowledge. You have to be honest. Take inventory. Ask yourself, "What is the real state of my life, business, faith, and relationships right now?" Then you must define where you want to go. Not where people expect you to go. Not what looks good on paper. But where your soul feels drawn. That vision becomes your internal compass. Without it, discipline becomes drudgery. With it, discipline becomes meaningful.

In my case, I knew I wanted to work in financial services. I saw the industry not just as a career, but as a vehicle for impact. I wasn't just selling products; I was offering peace of mind. I was protecting families. I was helping people make sense of their money. That purpose fueled my discipline. The mailroom wasn't beneath me; it was a training ground. Delivering envelopes became my ministry, my classroom. I paid attention. I studied the company's culture. I watched how people operated. I built relationships. All of it mattered. As I delivered those envelopes, I was delivering on my own destiny.

STAYING FOCUSED WHEN IT WOULD BE EASIER TO QUIT

Let me be honest. There were days when I wanted to give up. The grind was relentless. Appointments fell through. Clients said *no*. Some policies got canceled. Recruits gave up. Some months felt like I was taking one step forward, two steps back. The setbacks were real; so was the temptation to throw in the towel. Every time those thoughts crept in, I returned to Focused Discipline. I reminded myself: Decide what you want. Decide what you are willing to give up to get it. Set your mind. Get on with the work.

I'll say this to myself like a mantra. I would write it down. I'd recite it during my morning prayer. I'll review my goals. Then I'll take action again. This is what separates dreamers from doers. It's not the absence of discouragement. It's the presence of discipline. Discipline is the bridge between intention and execution. It's what keeps you in the game when your emotions tell you to walk away.

I moved from a sales rep to a District Manager, then to a Regional Manager, and finally to Regional Vice President in ten months—a position that often takes people five years. It wasn't due to a secret shortcut. It was due to a system. I had structure. I had Focused Discipline. I wasn't dabbling; I was determined.

NOT ABOUT PERFECTION, ABOUT PROGRESS

A lot of people confuse discipline with rigidity. They think it means never making mistakes or always getting it right. That's not what Focused Discipline is. It's not about having perfect days; it's about having purposeful days. Some days I missed goals. Some seasons were slower than others. I didn't let failure define me. I let it refine me. I evaluated. I adjusted. I kept showing up.

Consistency outweighs short-term excellence; disappearing for weeks undermines any initial success. Focused Discipline is about the long game. It's about building your life like a skyscraper, one floor at a time. Even now, decades into business and now pursuing ministry work, I use the same principles. I begin every day with prayer. I review my priorities. I plan my activities. I manage my focus. I refuse to let distractions lead me astray. You don't need to be perfect. You just need to be persistent.

FOCUSED DISCIPLINE

A TOOL FOR ANYONE, NOT JUST THE "TALENTED"

One of the greatest lies people believe is that success is for the "lucky few." You don't have to be born into wealth or gifted with charisma. I reject that entirely. What you need is Focused Discipline. I have mentored many people who had all the talent in the world, yet they couldn't stay consistent. I've also mentored others who started with nothing; they were hungry. They showed up. They learned. They grew. They stayed the course. They built something great.

You don't have to be the best to begin. You do have to begin to become the best. Discipline gives you the edge when talent alone won't cut it. Talent may open a door, but only discipline will keep you in the room. In every industry, the winners are not the flashiest. They are the most consistent, grounded, and focused. You can be that person.

THE SPIRITUAL BACKBONE

I must say this clearly: My strength comes from God. I believe in the power of prayer. I believe that discipline is spiritual. It is rooted in values. It is anchored in the Word. God has been my Chairman and CEO. In moments of discouragement, I don't just recite affirmations. I stand on promises. I believe Focused Discipline honors God; it means stewarding what He has placed in our hands. It means not wasting the gifts, time, and calling He has given. When we stay faithful, He does more with our obedience than we could do with our talent alone.

The Bible says in Romans 12:2, "Be ye transformed by the renewing of your mind." That's discipline. It's not a one-time event. It's daily. It's repetitive. It's intentional. I saturate my mornings with scripture. I remind myself that God is my source. I declare promises. I align my spirit. I trust that as I sow discipline, God will produce destiny.

REAL RESULTS, QUIET WINS

Focused Discipline helped me build businesses, train leaders, build a ministry, write books, mentor others, and keep my marriage strong. None of it was overnight. Its foundation was laid gradually—through time, persistence, and faith. I didn't get here because I was lucky. I got here because I showed up. Again. And again. And again.

If you want the results no one else has, you must be willing to do what no one else is willing to do. You must choose discipline over distraction. Commitment over convenience. Purpose over popularity. This chapter is not just about my story. It's about yours. You have a destiny to fulfill. You have people to impact. You have gifts that must be unwrapped. It will all begin when you choose to live a life of Focused Discipline.

SUMMARY: CHAPTER ONE—KEY TAKEAWAYS

- Focused Discipline is the consistent, quiet strength behind every meaningful achievement.

- It begins with knowing where you are and where you want to go.

- Discipline is not perfection; it is persistence.

- It requires sacrifice, structure, and a strong "why."

- Your talent doesn't matter if you don't show up. Discipline makes the difference.

- Root your discipline in God's promises and let prayer be your compass.

- Small actions, done daily, build big results over time.

- Consistency beats intensity over time; stay in the game.

- Discipline is a spiritual act; it's a form of worship and stewardship.

"Decide what you want. Decide what you are prepared to give up to get it. Set your mind on it. Get on with the work."

CHAPTER 2

THE POWER OF A CLEAR GOAL

"A goal without a plan is just a wish."
—ANTOINE DE SAINT-EXUPÉRY

IF FOCUSED DISCIPLINE IS THE ENGINE

If Focused Discipline is the engine, then a clear goal is the fuel. You can have the most disciplined mindset in the world, but if you're not pointed in the right direction, you'll only burn energy and time without going anywhere meaningful. Goals don't just guide action; they give your life direction, urgency, and meaning. Success, as I've come to know it, is not accidental. It's intentional. It's driven by clarity. Clarity about what matters most. Clarity about what you want. Clarity about who you want to become.

I've learned that without goals, people drift. They wake up each day with no target. When you have no target, you can't hit anything. A goal is more than just a wish; it's a decision backed by commitment. It's a spiritual contract between your present and your future self.

FROM DRIFT TO DRIVE

When I was still working my full-time job and building my business on the side, I knew exactly what I aimed for. I wanted to create a life where I could control my time, provide for my family, serve people, and live free from financial fear. I didn't just hope that would happen. I wrote it down. I set dates. I divided those goals into actionable steps across monthly, weekly, and daily intervals.

One of the most important lessons I learned early on is this: goals require deadlines. A dream without a date is just a fantasy. When I set the goal to become a Regional Vice President, I gave it a 12-month timeline. I made the commitment public. I structured my weekly calendar to reflect that goal. I reviewed it every single day. With God's help and focused action, I reached that goal in just 10 months. That was no accident. That was the power of a clear goal.

That single goal helped reshape the trajectory of my life. It changed how I used my mornings, how I structured my calls, and how I evaluated my wins and setbacks. A clear goal does something profound: it supports clearer, faster decision-making. When opportunities show up, you can ask, "Does this move me closer to or further from my goal?" That one question becomes your compass.

THE ANATOMY OF A GOAL

A real goal has five key traits. Let's break each one down:

1. It's Specific

Vague goals produce vague results. When you say, "I want to be successful," what does that actually mean? Does it mean earning a certain income? Building a certain kind of business? Buying your first home? Unless you get specific, your mind doesn't know what to focus on. A specific goal cuts through the noise. It brings precision to your vision. For example, instead of saying, "I want to grow spiritually," say, "I will spend 15 minutes every morning reading the Bible and praying." The more specific your goal, the more power it has.

2. It's Measurable

If you can't measure it, you can't manage it. Progress loves metrics. Track how far you've come and how far you still need to go. Whether it's tracking calls made, pounds lost, dollars saved, or chapters read, make it measurable. While working toward my promotion, I tracked every client interaction and monitored how many appointments I needed to meet my targets. That feedback loop helped me improve and adjust. Measuring brings visibility; visibility brings motivation.

3. It's Time-bound

A goal without a deadline is a moving target. Time frames create urgency and force you to act instead of delay. When I gave myself 12 months to hit a major milestone, it changed how I used my time each week. A timeline turns goals from someday into today. Even if you miss the deadline, the time-bound structure keeps you moving forward with purpose. Without time constraints, we drift; with them, we drive.

4. It's Personal

Your goal must matter to you—not your mentor, peers, or social media followers. If the goal isn't rooted in your values or calling, you won't stay committed. Personal goals anchor in your unique desires, needs, and dreams. When I set my early business goals, they were deeply personal; I wanted freedom for my family, security for our future, and the ability to serve others. That made quitting not an option. If the goal means something to you, you'll fight for it.

5. It's Written

Something powerful happens when you write down your goals. It's no longer just a thought; it becomes a declaration, a commitment, a roadmap. Studies show that written goals dramatically increase your chances of achievement. I wrote mine in journals, on sticky notes, even on bathroom mirrors. Why? I needed daily reminders. Written goals become visible, reviewable, and accountable. They move from the abstract to the concrete. If it's not written, it's easy to forget. When it's in front of you, it stays in focus.

SETTING GOALS

I remember clearly writing out my goals in a simple spiral notebook. One of them read, "Earn $100,000 within the next 12 months through my business." At the time, it sounded like a mountain. Once I wrote it down, it became real. Reviewing it made it achievable. Working toward it made it inevitable. If you want to achieve something significant, you need more than inspiration; you need structure. Goals give you that structure. They become the roadmap that turns intentions into outcomes.

THE SPIRITUAL SIDE OF GOAL SETTING

For me, goal setting holds no meaning outside of God's guidance. As believers, we don't just chase success; we pursue our God-given purpose. That means before you set a goal, pray. Ask God for wisdom, confirmation, and timing. Proverbs 16:3 says, "Commit your actions to the Lord, and your plans will succeed." That's not just a motivational quote; it's a divine principle.

My prayer life has been instrumental in every goal I've achieved. I pray over my list daily, asking God to bless the work of my hands and to align my goals with His will. Sometimes He adjusts them; sometimes He expands them. I always start with Him. There have been seasons where I pursued a goal that looked right on the outside but didn't sit right in my spirit. In prayer, God showed me that I was climbing the wrong mountain. That's why I say: don't just set goals; set God-aligned goals. When your goals align with God's plan, you don't just make progress; you bear fruit, operate with favor, and walk in peace. Even the setbacks make sense because you know you're in sync with a higher purpose.

CREATING MOMENTUM WITH MINI-GOALS

Big goals are essential, but they can feel overwhelming. That's why I believe in breaking goals into smaller, bite-sized targets—what I call mini-goals. Every big accomplishment in my life began as a series of small, focused steps. Want to grow your business? Set a goal to talk to five new prospects a day. Want to improve your health? Set a goal to walk 30 minutes each morning. Want to deepen your faith? Set a goal to read one chapter of Proverbs daily. These aren't complicated, but they're powerful.

Momentum is created by movement. Movement starts with clear, small steps you can repeat. These steps may seem minor on the surface, but they hold the power to shift your mindset, build habits, and fuel forward motion. Each mini-goal you complete reinforces the idea that progress is possible. You begin to trust yourself. You see evidence that you can follow through. That internal trust is essential for sustained success.

When you accomplish even a small win—like making a difficult phone call, finishing a workout, or waking up early to pray—your brain releases dopamine, the 'reward' chemical. That neurochemical reaction creates a feedback loop. Your brain says, "This feels good. Let's do more of it." That success signal builds belief, moving you from doubt to confidence and converting hesitation into action. As that belief grows, so does your momentum.

Mini-goals are like rungs on a ladder. You don't have to leap to the top; you just have to climb one step at a time.

Before you know it, you're standing in a place that once seemed unreachable. That's the power of compounding action. That's how empires are built—one faithful step at a time. In the early days of my career, I created daily checklists for myself. I would list small actions—calls to make, follow-ups to send, clients to visit. Checking them off brought me joy. It showed me that even on hard days, I was moving forward. Small steps matter.

GOALS AND ACCOUNTABILITY

One of the most powerful habits I built early in my career was goal review. I didn't just set goals and forget them. I reviewed them daily, weekly, and monthly. I had a partner in my wife—she played a key role in keeping me grounded and accountable. We planned together, celebrated wins together, and adjusted when things didn't go as planned. Accountability doesn't make you weak; it makes you wise. The more people you involve in your goals, the more rooted they become in your daily reality.

Share your goals with someone who believes in you and will remind you of them when you forget. Some of my biggest breakthroughs came after honest conversations with my wife. When I was discouraged, she reminded me why I started. When I slacked off, she lovingly called me higher. Her support turned my private goals into a shared mission. When we hit a goal, we celebrated together—sometimes with a special dinner, sometimes with a weekend getaway, other times just with a high-five and a prayer of thanks. Goals became not just a path to success, but a rhythm for our life together.

GOALS ARE NOT OPTIONAL

If you want to live with intention, goals are not optional; they are essential. Without them, time slips by. Years go by. Life moves, but you remain in place. Goals transform potential into progress. Too many people wait for clarity to arrive before they move. Here's the truth: clarity often comes after you start moving toward your goal, not before. Set the goal. Start walking. Let the path unfold.

Even now, decades into leadership and business, I still use a written goal list. I still pray over it. I still make adjustments. Every single day, I live by one truth: with goals, we create our destiny. You're not just a participant in life; you're a co-creator with God. One of the most powerful tools He has given you is the ability to set goals, pursue them with discipline, and shape a life that glorifies Him.

FOCUSED DISCIPLINE

WHEN GOALS FEEL OUT OF REACH

There will be days when your goals feel impossible. When nothing seems to be moving forward. When delays frustrate you. When doors close. On those days, don't abandon your goal; return to your why. Why did you set this goal? Why does it matter to you? What vision is tied to it? Sometimes your "why" will carry you when your motivation fades.

When you're tired, remember that rest is not failure. Take a breath. Recalibrate. Then keep going. God honors perseverance. He honors faithfulness. The road to your goal won't always be straight. With focused discipline and clear goals, it will lead somewhere worth going.

SUMMARY: CHAPTER TWO—KEY TAKEAWAYS

- A clear goal is essential to make discipline meaningful.

- Goals require specificity, deadlines, and personal importance.

- Written goals shape your decisions, emotions, and future.

- Prayer brings alignment between your goals and God's purpose.

- Break big goals into small, repeatable steps.

- Review and revisit your goals often.

- Accountability strengthens commitment.

- Without goals, progress is accidental; with goals, it becomes intentional.

- Goals simplify decision-making and fuel daily momentum.

- Even in delays or discouragement, your "why" will keep you going.

"With goals, we create our destiny."

CHAPTER 3

TIME IS LIFE

"Time is the currency of life; invest it wisely."
— UNKNOWN

THE VALUE OF TIME

There are 24 hours in a day. It's the one universal resource that no one can buy more of; no one can carry over into tomorrow. That's true for you, for me, and for every person who has ever accomplished anything great. It is the most democratically distributed asset on Earth. Every morning, we each receive the same deposit of 1,440 minutes. Unlike money, you can't save it. Unlike possessions, you can't pass it on. The rich can't hoard it; the poor aren't shortchanged. Everyone receives it equally.

Here's the defining truth: what you do with those 1,440 minutes makes the difference between a fruitful life and a frustrated one. It's not about how much time you have; it's about how much purpose you put into your time.

MASTERING ACTIVITIES

If time is equal for all of us, why are some people able to produce incredible results while others remain stuck? The answer is simple: successful people don't just manage time; they master their activities. They don't merely fill time; they focus time. They don't drift; they direct. This is where Focused Discipline enters the picture. It's the conscious, strategic commitment to fill your minutes with meaning, your days with direction, and your life with purpose. Focused Discipline is the bridge between intention and execution, between the vision in your mind and the legacy you want to leave.

Time itself cannot be managed. It cannot be paused, extended, or duplicated. What we can control is how we use it. That's where Focused Discipline becomes a game-changer. It transforms your schedule from something you chase into something you command. It elevates your calendar from chaos to clarity. It empowers you to stop reacting and start building. When you master your activities, you master your results. In the end, your schedule reflects your standards; your standards reflect your destiny.

TIME WILL PASS; WHAT WILL IT PRODUCE?

One of the most important mindset shifts I had to make was realizing that being busy is not the same as being productive. You can be in motion all day but still be going nowhere. Like a hamster on a wheel, a person can spin, sweat, and work from sunrise to sunset and still end the day with no measurable progress. I've met plenty of people who work all day, hustle nonstop, and still lie awake at night wondering why nothing seems to move forward. Motion doesn't always equal progress. Busyness without direction is just noise.

In my early career, I had to break away from the default rhythm of the culture around me. Instead of waking up and letting the day dictate my path, I decided to own my mornings. I began each day with prayer and reflection, anchoring myself in purpose. Then I wrote down the key activities that aligned with my goals. Not everything made the list; only what mattered most. That clarity saved me from the tyranny of the urgent.

I structured my time not around hours but around impact. I asked myself: What will move the needle today? What interaction, phone call, or decision will draw me closer to the vision I carry in my heart? That simple yet powerful discipline of intentional living elevated the quality of my days. I no longer lived in reaction; I lived in purpose. My schedule included time blocks for spiritual disciplines, physical wellness, relational investments, and strategic business activities. I began to treat my time the way a builder treats blueprints: with precision, purpose, and patience.

Time will pass regardless. The question is, what will it produce? If you don't plan your hours with intentionality, they will be consumed by distraction. Distractions are the silent killers of destiny. They don't shout; they whisper. They nudge. They offer just enough dopamine to keep you satisfied but never enough to help you grow. They chip away at your focus like waves against a rock, wearing down your edge until you're left dull and disengaged. Before you know it, the day is gone, and the goals are untouched. The calendar is full, but the soul is empty. That's why time mastery isn't optional; it's essential. Every minute matters when your destiny is on the line.

ACTIVITIES CREATE OUTCOMES

What you do in your hours determines what your hours produce. Time itself is neutral. Your choices within that time create excellence or mediocrity. As the saying goes, "Don't prioritize your schedule; schedule your priorities." Every morning, I created a simple checklist. I wrote down who I needed to call, follow up with, serve, or meet. I didn't just guess; I tracked. Over time, this built clarity. I began to notice which activities brought the most results and which drained time without return.

For example, I realized that prospecting in the morning gave me better energy. I learned that double-booking Monday set the tone for my entire week. I found that client follow-ups were more effective after 5 PM. These patterns became habits. Those habits became results. Don't let time just happen to you. Make your time obey you. Discipline in activity creates dignity in outcome. You build confidence not just by achieving results but by knowing that your actions are aligned with your values and goals. That is the power of daily disciplines; done well, they create a life of excellence.

THE MYTH OF MULTITASKING

If you want to master your time, you must reject the myth of multitasking. We live in a culture obsessed with doing multiple things at once: juggling phone calls while replying to emails, listening to podcasts while scrolling social media, and attending meetings while answering texts. At first glance, it seems productive. It feels efficient. The research is clear: multitasking reduces efficiency, weakens focus, and significantly increases the likelihood of mistakes.

FOCUSED DISCIPLINE

The human brain isn't wired to do multiple complex tasks simultaneously. Instead, it switches rapidly between tasks. That switching may feel like multitasking, but in truth, it fragments our attention. Every time your focus shifts, even briefly, it takes precious seconds to regain the mental traction you lost. Those seconds add up. Over time, they erode both productivity and peace.

Multitasking doesn't just waste time; it creates stress. It diminishes the quality of our conversations, our work, and our relationships. It robs us of being fully present. In pursuit of doing everything at once, we often end up doing nothing well. I had to learn this lesson the hard way. Early in my career, I prided myself on how much I could "handle" at once. I routinely managed calls while commuting to appointments, addressed messages, and planned the following day amidst the demands of the current moment. Over time, I began to notice the cost. My effectiveness dropped. My interactions felt shallow. I missed key moments with clients; even more painful, with my family.

That's when I made a decision: to live and work with presence. I chose to give my full attention to one task at a time. When I was on a call, I was fully present. When I was in a meeting, I listened; really listened. When I was with my family, I silenced notifications and engaged with them fully. That focused presence became a discipline. That discipline became a gift. What I discovered was profound: the more present I became, the more powerful my results. The deeper my connections. The higher the quality of my work. Focus wasn't just good for business; it was healing for the soul.

Multitasking divides your focus; discipline unites it. Your life begins to shift when you give your whole self to one thing at a time. That's where excellence lives: in the undivided moment. In a world constantly tugging at your attention, Focused Discipline gives you the power to say, "I'm here, fully."

WHY ROUTINES MATTER

Routines are powerful because they automate discipline. When you have a strong routine, you no longer rely on motivation. You don't have to wonder if you feel like doing something; you do it because it's woven into your daily rhythm. It becomes automatic. Just like brushing your teeth or tying your shoes, these behaviors become part of your identity.

For me, my routine starts with prayer and gratitude. It centers me spiritually and emotionally before I enter the day's demands. Then I move into my checklist: my intentional to-do list that reflects what matters most. I track my goals, follow up with key clients, and review what's working and what isn't. I go to the gym in the afternoon to reset my mind and strengthen my body. I spend quality time with my wife in the evening and prep for the next day before bed. These practices keep my mind clear, my heart focused, and my mission alive.

These routines weren't built in a day. They were built over time, through trial, error, and intentional alignment with my priorities. I didn't always get it right; I stuck with it. Over time, those daily choices became a framework of stability. Now, they serve as rails that keep my life moving forward, especially during unpredictable seasons. A routine is not bondage: it's freedom. It frees your mind to focus on results, not logistics. It gives structure to your time and substance to your day. It reduces decision fatigue and makes space for what truly matters.

Here's why routines are so powerful:

1. They Reduce Mental Clutter

You don't waste energy deciding what to do next. Your day flows with intentionality.

2. They Protect Your Priorities

A routine helps you schedule what matters before life crowds it out.

3. They Foster Momentum

Small, repeated actions compound into big results over time.

4. They Build Confidence

When you consistently follow through on your routine, you reinforce belief in your ability to achieve your goals.

5. They Strengthen Resilience

In stressful seasons, your routine becomes a life raft; it keeps you grounded and focused.

6. They Align Your Habits With Your Purpose

Every repeated action is a vote for the person you're becoming.

If you want to live a disciplined life, build disciplined routines. Start small. Be consistent. Watch how your day—and your destiny—begin to transform.

MAKING TIME OBEY YOU

People often say, "I don't have enough time." The truth is, we all have time for what we make time for. The key is to take authority over your calendar. Don't be passive with your schedule. Take dominion over it.

I used to let other people's emergencies dictate my day. I'd jump from one task to another, feeling rushed and reactive. Focused Discipline taught me to live by design, not by default. Now, when I plan my week, I schedule the big things first: faith, family, follow-through. I don't let distractions creep in and steal what matters. When interruptions come (and they always do), I adjust; I don't abandon the mission.

Planning is not optional for the disciplined life. If you don't plan your day, someone else will. Your email inbox, your phone notifications, your social media feeds—they're all ready to run your schedule. A focused person says, "No, I'm running this day."

THE WISDOM OF H.L. HUNT

One quote that changed my life came from businessman H.L. Hunt: "Decide what you want. Decide what you are prepared to give up to get it. Set your mind and get on with the work." This is a blueprint for mastering your time.

First, clarify your goal. Then identify the cost. Commit. Finally, execute—daily. You don't need more hours. You need more intention. There's always a cost to your goals. The question is not whether you'll sacrifice; it's what you'll sacrifice. Will you sacrifice purpose for comfort? Or comfort for purpose? Will you give your time to what matters most or to what matters least?

The most fulfilled people I know are not the ones with the most talent. They are the ones with the most intention. They live on purpose. They act with clarity. They protect their time like treasure.

FAITH AND TIME

I believe managing your activities is not just a success principle: it's a spiritual act. The Bible says, "Teach us to number our days, that we may gain a heart of wisdom" (Psalm 90:12). Every day is a gift. Every minute is a seed. Every hour has eternal significance.

That's why I don't waste time arguing, procrastinating, or getting stuck in self-pity. I go to God for direction, then I get to work. One of the ways I honor God is by honoring my time. I invite Him into my calendar. I pray over my weekly plan. I ask for wisdom on what to say *yes* to—and strength to say *no* when needed. That's part of spiritual maturity: recognizing that not every good thing is a God thing. Focused time is a form of worship. God created time, and He expects us to steward it.

Just as we tithe our finances, we should also be intentional with our hours. That doesn't mean we never rest. Rest is holy. Even rest must be intentional, not passive.

PRACTICAL TOOLS FOR TIME MASTERY

Here are a few tools that have helped me:

1. **Daily Success Checklist:** A short list of 5–7 things I must do each day to move my business forward.

2. **The Sunday Planning Hour:** Every Sunday evening, I plan the week ahead: appointments, priorities, prayer targets.

3. **Time Blocking:** I group similar tasks together and schedule blocks for deep work, follow-ups, and personal growth.

No List: I keep a list of things I say *no* to in this season: projects, distractions, requests that don't align with my mission.

These tools aren't magic, but they keep me grounded. They remind me that success is not a result of chance: it's the outcome of choices.

SUMMARY: CHAPTER THREE—KEY TAKEAWAYS

- Time itself can't be managed, but activities can.
- Prioritize actions that produce the greatest impact.
- Create daily checklists to maintain clarity and control.
- Routines automate discipline and reduce wasted energy.
- Reject multitasking; focus on one thing at a time.
- Own your schedule; don't let others dictate your priorities.
- Make time for what matters most: God, family, growth, service.
- Use time as a tool to fulfill your purpose.
- Planning is spiritual; invite God into your calendar.
- Small actions, executed daily, create lasting results.

"Decide what you want. Decide what you are prepared to give up to get it. Set your mind and get on with the work."

CHAPTER 4

SELF-IMAGE AND PERSONAL SUCCESS

"Whether you think you can or you think you can't, you're right."
—HENRY FORD

MASTERING YOUR BELIEF

Before you can master your business, you must master your belief. Every decision you make, every goal you chase, every risk you take—all of it is filtered through the lens of what you believe about yourself. Belief is the engine that drives discipline; discipline is the vehicle that delivers results. If your belief is weak, your execution will suffer, no matter how ambitious your intentions may be. The foundation of belief begins with how you see yourself.

THE IMPORTANCE OF SELF-IMAGE

Self-image isn't just a psychological concept; it's a spiritual reality. It is the internal thermostat that sets the climate of your life. If it's set too low, you'll constantly sabotage your efforts to rise higher. If it's set with clarity, strength, and alignment with purpose, you will begin to operate with consistency and courage. Self-image is the invisible portrait you carry inside. It determines how you respond to opportunities: whether you shrink or show up. It defines how you handle challenges: whether you retreat or rise. It affects how you view others: whether you collaborate confidently or compare constantly. In short, how you see yourself is the silent script that shapes every visible outcome.

Many people fail not due to a lack of talent, resources, or opportunity, but due to an internal ceiling. They operate with unconscious limits. They say the right things outwardly yet struggle inwardly with unworthiness. Progress gets sabotaged because, deep down, they don't see themselves as worthy, capable, or called to succeed. They misinterpret favor as luck, open doors as coincidences, and challenges as disqualification. That's why Focused Discipline must begin on the inside. What happens inside of you will always manifest outside of you. Your habits, relationships, leadership, and even your income will eventually reflect your self-image. No sustainable transformation happens apart from internal renovation. If you want to change your life, you must first change your narrative. You must rewrite the story that plays in your head; that story will become your strategy, your standard, and ultimately, your success.

SELF-IMAGE: THE GOVERNOR OF YOUR LIFE

I often say, "Your self-image is the governor of your life." Just like a governor on an engine limits its speed, your self-image sets a limit on how far you'll go in life. It doesn't matter how much training you receive, how many opportunities come your way, or how passionate you are; if your inner image doesn't support your vision, you will find a way to sabotage or shrink back. You'll hesitate instead of stepping forward. You'll doubt instead of deciding. You'll defer instead of deliver.

This is why some people stay stuck despite being surrounded by growth environments. They attend conferences, read books, and watch motivational videos; if deep inside they still see themselves as unworthy, incapable, or broken, they'll keep hitting a ceiling. That ceiling is not external: it's internal. The mind won't allow the body to operate beyond what it believes is possible. The heart won't pursue what it doesn't think it deserves. If you see yourself as mediocre, no matter how much success you taste, you will self-correct back to average. You'll think, "This is too good to be true," and unconsciously begin to sabotage it. If you see yourself as a failure, even breakthroughs will feel like accidents; you'll dismiss them instead of stewarding them.

If you see yourself as someone chosen, equipped, and growing, you will begin to live like it. You'll lean into responsibility. You'll take bolder steps. You'll persevere through resistance because you believe that what's ahead is consistent with who you are inside. That's how transformation begins. It starts not in striving but in seeing: seeing yourself differently, seeing your purpose clearly, and seeing your life through the lens of God's promises. Your life will never rise above the image you carry within. You may experience temporary success, but it will never feel sustainable until it aligns with how you see yourself.

THE IMPACT OF BELIEF ON SUCCESS

This explains why people with the same credentials can have drastically different outcomes. Two individuals may have the same education, mentorship, and exposure, yet one will multiply what they're given while the other barely maintains. Why? One believes in themselves; the other is constantly second-guessing. One moves with conviction, while the other hesitates. The results follow belief. Not just belief in God, but belief in who God says you are. Romans 12:2 says, "Be transformed by the renewing of your mind." Notice it doesn't say be changed by chance or transformed by hustle. It doesn't say transformation comes from performance. True change is the product of a renewed inner life. It's not just about doing different things; it's about becoming a different person from the inside out.

MY JOURNEY WITH SELF-IMAGE

When I first arrived in the United States, I had a strong vision but limited external credentials. I wasn't the most educated. I didn't have a strong network. I began in the mailroom. I refused to see myself as "just a mailroom worker." I saw myself as someone preparing for leadership. I walked into every office floor with my head up, spirit alert, and goals in front of me. I remember delivering mail to executives and decision-makers with respect and quiet confidence. I wasn't just handing them envelopes; I was preparing to take my place at the table. I took mental notes on how they spoke, how they presented themselves, and how they operated. I studied excellence from the inside out.

Eventually, that inner image became outer evidence. Within months, I moved from the mailroom to an analyst position. Later, I became a leader, a business owner, and a pastor. None of that would have happened if I hadn't first seen myself differently. The outer results were simply catching up to the inner vision.

FOCUSED DISCIPLINE

HOW TO RENEW YOUR INNER IMAGE

Changing your self-image is not magic. It's intentional. It doesn't happen overnight, but it can begin in a moment: right now, as you read this. The process starts with awareness, followed by intentional practice. Here are the key disciplines that helped me:

1. Speak What You Believe, Not Just What You See

Words are creative forces. Every morning, I declared out loud: "I am focused. I am chosen. I am disciplined. I am called to lead." Even before my reality reflected those words, I spoke them. Why? Because your words are seeds. If you plant them consistently, they produce a harvest of identity.

2. Feed Your Mind with Growth

I committed to becoming a lifelong learner. I read books that stretched my thinking, watched content that educated and inspired me, and engaged in conversations that lifted my mindset. Growth doesn't happen by accident; it happens by design.

3. Filter Out Toxic Inputs

You can't absorb constant negativity and still expect to thrive with a positive mindset. I chose to distance myself from discouraging conversations and environments that weakened my faith or self-belief. I became intentional about what I allowed my eyes to see and ears to hear; they shape thoughts and energy.

4. Meditate on God's Promises

Scriptures like "I can do all things through Christ who strengthens me" became daily declarations. I didn't just read them; I spoke them, believed them, and built my self-image upon them. The Word of God became the mirror in which I saw who I truly was.

5. Act in Alignment with the Person You're Becoming

Before I ever had a title, I carried the mindset. I dressed like a leader. I prepared like a professional. I showed up on time. Excellence became my standard: not because of position, but because of identity.

THE ROLE OF FAITH IN IDENTITY

The world will always try to define you by your past, your failures, or your limitations. God defines you by His Word. Your sense of self should be grounded in something deeper and more meaningful than what others think, feel, or say. You must root it in truth. When God calls someone, He doesn't consult their background. He speaks to their potential. That's how David became king. That's how Gideon became a warrior. That's how you rise; not by trying harder, but by believing better. Your success begins in your spirit. Before you build wealth, influence, or impact, you must build an inner image consistent with God's promises. Otherwise, you'll keep sabotaging your next level.

Let me be clear: this isn't about arrogance or blind confidence. It's about spiritual agreement. When your beliefs align with God's Word, you begin to walk in divine rhythm. You stop striving to prove yourself and start showing up with peace and power. Faith allows you to stand tall even when life knocks you down. It reminds you that your value is not in your performance but in your purpose. A faith-based self-image gives you the stability to handle success and the resilience to grow through setbacks.

BREAK THE CYCLE OF SELF-SABOTAGE

Have you ever seen someone achieve a breakthrough and then lose it? That's self-image at work. If your inner story contradicts your outer reality, you'll unconsciously find ways to return to what's familiar. That's why so many people win temporarily, yet not sustainably. You must upgrade the story you tell yourself. Interrupt old patterns that whisper, "You don't belong here," or "This won't last." Those thoughts are not facts; they are scripts, and they can be rewritten.

To break the cycle, you must:

1. Raise your self-expectation. You will never rise above the level you expect of yourself. Low expectations produce low engagement, low effort, and low results. Raising your self-expectation means refusing to settle. It's making the decision to live at a higher standard—not due to pressure, but for purpose. Begin to expect growth, expect the best, and accept responsibility. Expect to be a person of excellence and follow-through. Expectation is the spark that ignites transformation.

2. Upgrade your mental dialogue.

THE POWER OF INNER DIALOGUE

The words you speak to yourself are more influential than anything spoken by others. Inner dialogue becomes destiny. If your self-talk is filled with doubt, defeat, and delay, your outcomes will match. Replacing negative mental scripts with faith-filled truth is essential. Say things like: "I am growing. I am qualified. I am anointed for this assignment." Monitor your inner speech as if it were a coaching session—because it is.

FOCUSED DISCIPLINE

SURROUND YOURSELF WITH PEOPLE WHO SEE YOUR GREATNESS

Your environment influences your self-image. Being around people who constantly point out your flaws will drain your confidence. Surrounding yourself with individuals who challenge, affirm, and inspire you will elevate your self-image. Seek mentors who speak life into your potential. Build friendships that celebrate growth. Let others remind you of who you are becoming when you momentarily forget.

PRACTICE DAILY DECLARATIONS OF FAITH AND FOCUS

Your declarations are daily investments in your mindset. Speak out loud the truth of who you are and what you're becoming. These affirmations are not self-hype: they are alignment tools. They center your heart and clarify your path. Write a few statements grounded in Scripture and repeat them each morning. Declarations discipline your thoughts and establish identity in truth rather than circumstance.

SELF-IMAGE GROWS THROUGH ACTION

Self-image grows through action. Every time you take a bold step—even a small one—you expand your belief about what's possible. You prove to yourself that you're not trapped by fear. Whether it's having a difficult conversation, launching a new project, or showing up to a meeting with confidence, these small risks build emotional and spiritual muscle. Over time, courage compounds. Each of these steps reinforces the next. They work together to raise your identity, reset your expectations, and rewire your responses. This is not a one-time fix; it's a lifelong habit.

As you do the work, you'll watch your life rise to meet your renewed self-image. Every time you show up with integrity, take a step outside your comfort zone, or keep going when you want to quit, you're rewriting your internal script. Discipline isn't just about doing; it's about believing while doing.

THE IMAGE YOU PROJECT

Your self-image not only affects how you see yourself; it influences how others respond to you. Confidence is magnetic. Clarity is attractive. When you carry yourself with focus and discipline, people take notice. Clients trust you. Teams follow you. Doors open. The energy you bring into a room communicates more than your words ever could. You either project assurance or uncertainty. People may not be able to articulate it, but they feel it.

That's why it's essential to cultivate the image within—not for vanity, but for effectiveness. This is not about pretending. It's about presenting. You present the best version of who you're becoming. Lead with authenticity, grounded in faith and fueled by discipline. You don't have to be perfect. You must be present. Presence comes from clarity.

When your inner image aligns with your God-given identity, you stop playing small. You stop shrinking in the face of opportunity. You stop apologizing for excellence. You show up with authority—not due to ego, but because of assignment. You're not trying to impress; you're trying to impact. That's the shift. That's the fruit of Focused Discipline.

SUMMARY: CHAPTER FOUR—KEY TAKEAWAYS

- Self-image determines how far you go in life.
- True transformation starts from within, not just with action.
- What you believe about yourself will shape how you behave.
- Daily declarations, spiritual discipline, and mental renewal are essential.
- Root your identity in God's truth, not public opinion.
- Self-sabotage ends when self-image aligns with purpose.
- Confidence isn't arrogance; it's agreement with who God says you are.
- A focused inner image leads to focused external results.

"As a man thinks in his heart, so is he." (Proverbs 23:7)

CHAPTER 5

KNOW YOUR WHY

"He who has a why to live can bear almost anyhow."
—FRIEDRICH NIETZSCHE

If discipline is the engine that keeps you moving, purpose is the fuel that keeps you motivated. You can have all the strategies, skills, and resources in the world, but lacking a deep and personal reason to keep going will eventually fade your momentum. Purpose breathes life into discipline. It transforms hard work into holy work. It converts duty into devotion. The question is not just what you're doing, but why you're doing it. Without a compelling "why," even the most talented individuals burn out. Without a meaningful purpose, it's easy to get lost in busyness and confuse movement with progress. With a strong sense of purpose, even the most ordinary person can achieve extraordinary things.

Purpose ignites passion, sustains energy, and anchors your direction when distractions arise. People don't quit due to weakness. They quit when they've lost sight of their reason for pressing on. Motivation fades. Emotions shift. External rewards can take time. Your "why" is the deep well you draw from when everything else runs dry. It's the unshakable reason behind your routine. The force behind your follow-through. That's why, in the journey of Focused Discipline, knowing your why is non-negotiable. It serves as your compass, anchor, and power source. Your why reminds you of who you are, who you're helping, and what legacy you're building. It re-centers you when life tries to pull you off course. Without it, discipline becomes dry. It becomes a checklist with no meaning, a grind with no heart. With it, discipline becomes destiny. Purpose gives your efforts eternal value and turns the mundane into the meaningful.

PURPOSE DRIVES PERSISTENCE

There were seasons in my life when everything around me said, "Stop." Financial pressure. Long nights. Slow results. Disappointment. People walking away. I'll be honest, quitting sounded reasonable more than once, but I didn't quit. Not because it was easy. Not due to talent. I didn't quit because I knew my why. I was fighting for something bigger than comfort. I was building a future for my family. I was helping others find security and peace of mind. I was honoring the call God had placed on my life. That clarity kept me focused. I would remind myself: "If I give up now, who else might I be letting down? Whose breakthrough might be delayed because I stopped short?" Knowing my why kept me accountable not just to myself, but to the mission entrusted to me.

When you know your why, you develop the ability to endure what others escape. You keep going, not because it feels good, but because it matters. Your purpose will keep you steady in the storm. It becomes the internal voice that says, "Not yet, there's more to be done."

DISCOVERING YOUR WHY

Your why isn't always obvious at first. It's not something you stumble upon by accident or hear in a motivational video. It is something revealed through reflection, experiences, pain, passion, and purpose. Sometimes it's born out of disappointment. Sometimes it emerges in a quiet moment of prayer. Other times, it takes shape slowly—like a puzzle, one piece at a time. Discovering your why requires stillness. It requires self-honesty. It often requires revisiting your journey to find the themes that have guided you, even when you weren't aware of them. Many people never find their why because they're too busy to stop and reflect. Reflection is not a waste of time; it is the foundation of purposeful time.

FOCUSED DISCIPLINE

Here are a few questions to help uncover your why:

- What problem do I feel most passionate about solving?

- What impact do I want to make in people's lives?

- What injustice do I feel compelled to challenge?

- What legacy do I want to leave behind?

- What breaks my heart or lights my fire?

- What brings me joy even when I'm not being paid?

- When have I felt most alive, most fulfilled, most in flow?

As you dig into these questions, patterns emerge. You begin to see your values. You notice recurring passions. You recognize the moments that moved you most and why they did. You find what energizes you beyond money or recognition. From there, your why becomes clearer. Not because someone gave it to you, but because it was always inside of you, waiting to be uncovered. Sometimes your why is rooted in pain. Maybe you grew up with scarcity; now you help others build financial security. Perhaps you were once overlooked or rejected; now you make it your mission to see and uplift others.

You may have experienced a tragedy; now your life is committed to bringing healing or awareness. Your past may not define you, but it can direct you.

Other times, your why comes from deep joy. You may love teaching, empowering, building, or serving. It could be your natural gifts, your spiritual calling, or your unique way of adding value to others. Whatever it is, let it be real. Don't manufacture it. Don't copy someone else's. The most powerful why is the most authentic one. Remember, your why can evolve. As you grow, your vision may grow. As you mature, your impact may shift. Stay open. Stay aligned. Stay honest. Your why must come from within. When it does, it will stand strong when pressure rises. It will outlast seasons, setbacks, and self-doubt. It will give your Focused Discipline direction, durability, and divine meaning.

PURPOSE OVER PROFITS

Let me be clear: making money is not a bad thing. Money is a tool; we all need it to sustain our families, invest in others, and fulfill our vision. If your only motivation is financial gain, you will eventually run out of steam. Why? Money can't fulfill your soul. Purpose must come before profits. If profit is your only driver, you will compromise your values. When purpose is your motivator, profit becomes a byproduct, not the goal.

I've met many entrepreneurs who hit a six- or seven-figure milestone and still felt empty. Why? They were chasing numbers, not meaning. There were times in my journey when I didn't see immediate financial reward. Yet I kept showing up. I kept putting in the work. I kept following up with clients. I kept mentoring and building. I believed in the mission. Helping families prepare for the future was more than a transaction: it was a transformation. That belief became my fuel. It kept me grounded. It kept me humble. It kept me hungry. Focused Discipline that flows from purpose produces fulfillment. When your work is connected to something eternal, even the hard days become worth it.

WHY FAITH FUELS PURPOSE

For me, my ultimate why is rooted in faith. Faith is not an accessory to purpose; it is the foundation. I believe I was created by God with intention, on purpose, and for a purpose. That truth reshapes everything. It informs how I live, how I work, and how I respond to challenges. I'm not just building a business; I'm fulfilling a divine assignment. I'm not just providing a service; I'm meeting a spiritual need. Every interaction, every client, and every goal becomes part of something sacred.

When you know that God has placed you on this earth for a reason, you no longer live for validation. You live for impact. You stop asking, "Do people approve of what I'm doing?" and start asking, "Am I being faithful to what God entrusted to me?" That's the power of a faith-fueled purpose; it anchors you in eternal truth even when temporal outcomes waver. This belief system transformed how I view success. Success isn't just about reaching goals; it's about obeying the God who gave the goals. It's about stewarding time, gifts, and opportunities in a way that honors Him. Faith brings dimension to purpose. It lifts your vision from earthly ambition to eternal significance. Purpose becomes deeper when it's anchored in your relationship with God. It's not just about what you want to do; it's about what you're called to do. Calling gives your purpose authority. It means your path has been assigned, and your progress is backed by heaven. That changes how you approach your work. You no longer grind out of desperation. You move with confidence, knowing that grace goes before you.

HOW YOUR WHY CHANGES THE WAY YOU WORK

When your why is strong, your how gets sharper. You show up earlier. You stay later. You prepare more intentionally. You recover faster from setbacks. You say *no* to what distracts and *yes* to what aligns. Purpose brings focus. Here's how a strong why influences your day:

- You stop procrastinating. When something matters deeply, you don't delay; you dive in.

- You embrace discomfort. When your goal is big enough, the pain becomes part of the process.

- You grow more resilient. Setbacks don't stop you; they refine you.

- You lead with conviction. People feel your passion when you're anchored in purpose.

- You live with direction. Your calendar, energy, and decisions align with a mission.

Purpose is not a motivational slogan. It's a practical strategy. It brings structure and spirit to everything you do.

LEGACY AND LONG-TERM THINKING

Your why is not just about today. It's about tomorrow. It's about your children, your clients, your community, and your calling. Purpose pulls you into the future while keeping you rooted in your values. I've often asked myself: What will outlive me because I stayed focused? What will remain when I'm gone? Will others be better, stronger, and more equipped because I refused to quit? Your why gives meaning to the sacrifices. It gives weight to the hours. It turns ordinary work into eternal impact. That's the beauty of Focused Discipline: it takes purpose and translates it into motion.

Never underestimate the power of a deep why. It's stronger than talent. Stronger than pressure. Stronger than fatigue. Purpose gives you permission to keep going when logic says stop. If you don't know your why yet, seek it. Pray for it. Ask questions. Reflect. When you find it, write it down. Revisit it often. Let it shape your decisions and energize your discipline.

SUMMARY: CHAPTER FIVE—KEY TAKEAWAYS

- Purpose is the fuel behind long-term discipline.

- Without a strong why, even talented people burn out.

- Knowing your why helps you push through obstacles and discouragement.

- Purpose is discovered through reflection, passion, and pain.

- Focused Discipline without a purpose becomes routine without meaning.

- Your why should be bigger than money; it should serve people and glorify God.

- A faith-rooted purpose gives you peace, power, and direction.

- Purpose clarifies your priorities and strengthens your endurance.

"Success is not about being driven; it's about being drawn by purpose."

Knowing your why fuels perseverance. Take a moment to list the reasons your goal matters. Who will be impacted when you succeed? Let that motivation sustain you when discipline feels hard.

CHAPTER 6

DESIRE, DETERMINATION, AND DISCIPLINE

"Success is not final, failure is not fatal: it is the courage to continue that counts."
—WINSTON CHURCHILL

Every significant achievement begins with desire. Not a shallow wish or fleeting emotion, but a deep inner fire that says, "There's more for me." This isn't the kind of desire that fades at the first sign of difficulty: it's the type that stirs you from within, keeps you awake at night with possibilities, and pulls you forward when logic says stay still. It's the desire that doesn't go away after a bad day or a failed attempt. This kind of desire is rooted in conviction. It awakens a sense of divine restlessness that won't allow you to settle for less than what you were created for. It disrupts your comfort and ignites your calling.

Before discipline becomes a habit and before consistency becomes a strength, something must spark the journey; that spark is desire. Desire is the internal alarm clock that wakes you up earlier, the hidden engine that pushes you to take risks, and the unseen force behind every dream worth chasing. It fuels vision, shapes priorities, and creates momentum. Desire gives you the courage to start, the vision to endure, and the fire to rise after every fall. It reminds you that there is something greater ahead if you will press forward.

Desire is what gets you started. Determination is what keeps you going. Discipline transforms both into results. These three forces, when aligned, form the core of Focused Discipline. You cannot sustain greatness on discipline alone if there is no desire driving it. Without desire, discipline becomes duty without direction. Desire without determination is powerless: it fizzles out at the first sign of resistance. When all three work together, progress becomes unstoppable. You don't just move; you move with clarity, consistency, and conviction. That's how dreams turn into outcomes and visions into impact.

THE POWER OF DESIRE

Desire is the birthplace of all change. It wakes you up early. It pushes you to study, stretch, and sacrifice. It drives the athlete to train when no one is watching. It moves the entrepreneur to keep building even when the numbers don't add up. It stirs the leader to cast vision even when no one yet believes. It's not always loud, but it is persistent. Desire works in the background, whispering, "Keep going. Keep growing. Don't stop here."

Not all desire is equal. Some desires are selfish, impulsive, or born out of comparison. That kind of desire can lead to burnout or bitterness. True desire, the kind that fuels destiny, aligns with purpose. It doesn't fade with resistance: it grows stronger in adversity. It is not rooted in envy but in clarity. It's not about proving someone wrong: it's about fulfilling something right. It doesn't just want success but to make a difference.

Desire says, "I want to make a difference." Desire says, "I can do better than this." Desire says, "There's something bigger inside of me." This kind of desire isn't loud; it's relentless. It won't let you settle. It shows up in your restlessness when you know you were made for more. It lives in your discomfort with mediocrity. If you feed it, it can change your entire life. It will shape how you speak, how you move, and what you allow. It will pull you toward environments, relationships, and routines that stretch you.

So how do you cultivate this kind of desire? First, you must be honest. You must ask, "What do I really want, and why?" Then, surround yourself with people and environments that elevate your vision. Read books that challenge your thinking. Listen to voices that stir your spirit. Pray and ask God to reveal what He placed in you. Desire doesn't grow in isolation; it grows in the presence of vision. The more clearly you see what's possible, the more deeply you'll want to pursue it.

A STORY OF SPARK AND STAGNATION

I once mentored a young man who had all the tools: charisma, intelligence, and connections. After months of training and encouragement, he still hadn't made a single move. When I sat with him, I asked what was holding him back. He said plainly, "I just don't have the desire." That conversation deeply marked me. It reminded me that no matter how many resources you offer someone, nothing replaces internal drive. No amount of coaching can compensate for the absence of desire.

Without it, people stay stuck, full of potential but empty of purpose. Like a high-performance car with no gas in the tank, they look the part but can't go anywhere. That's what happens to many people. They're not lazy; they're unclear. They've been talked out of their passion. They've forgotten why they started. Or they never gave themselves permission to dream in the first place. Somewhere along the way, they replaced boldness with busyness and fire with fear.

That's why it's essential to reconnect with what fuels you. What makes you come alive? What problems stir your compassion? What dreams won't leave you alone? Desire can be stirred. It can be reignited through exposure to vision, reflection on what matters most, spiritual encounters with God that remind you of who you are, and small wins that rebuild confidence. Sometimes, all it takes is one moment of clarity to change everything. Desire is not a gift reserved for a few; it's a decision to want more. That desire becomes fuel. Fuel for excellence. Fuel for impact. Fuel for discipline. Without it, you'll drag through life. With it, you'll run your race with joy.

DETERMINATION: THE DECISION TO KEEP GOING

Desire gets you off the starting blocks; determination gets you across the finish line. Determination is desire with a backbone. It's the decision to press on when the feelings fade. It's waking up and showing up even when nothing is exciting. It's the silent resolve to keep going when the applause is gone. Determination doesn't need attention: it thrives on commitment.

Determination says:

- "I will not quit."
- "I will get back up."
- "I will outlast the delay."

Determination is not about drama; it's about daily decisions. It's about choosing to follow through on your commitments long after the mood in which you made them has passed. It's not driven by hype but by honor— honor for your calling, family, and future. People often mistake motivation for determination. Motivation is emotional. Determination is foundational. It is built on values, not vibes.

I've seen people with less talent go further than their gifted peers simply because they refused to quit. They weren't always the flashiest. They didn't always have the perfect background. But they had resolve. That resolve earned them results. Consistency consistently outperforms charisma when pressure comes. Determination is forged in resistance. It grows stronger every time you don't give up. It earns you the credibility that talent alone cannot. It is the bridge between temporary setbacks and long-term success. It allows you to show up on the bad days, speak life over dry seasons, and keep watering the dream even when there's no sign of rain.

If desire is what wakes you up, determination is what helps you rise again after you've been knocked down. It keeps you standing when others sit, and pushing when others pause. It is not optional: it is essential.

DISCIPLINE: TURNING DESIRE INTO DESTINY

Discipline is what turns desire and determination into destiny. Without discipline, desire remains a wish, and determination fades into frustration. When you add structure to your pursuit, everything changes. Discipline is the difference between wanting and becoming. It's the tool that shapes the raw material of potential into the masterpiece of purpose.

Discipline gives your desire a container. It gives your determination a compass. It helps you measure, track, and progress. Discipline doesn't wait for feelings; it follows a plan. It transforms good intentions into consistent execution. It provides a framework to keep moving even when the road gets rocky.

Discipline says:

FOCUSED DISCIPLINE

- "I will wake up and plan my day."
- "I will stick to the process even when it's boring."
- "I will do what needs to be done, not just what I feel like doing."

In my own life, I've seen discipline turn average days into productive ones. It has carried me through seasons of doubt. It has helped me keep promises to myself. When desire was dim and progress felt slow, discipline kept me moving forward. It is the quiet companion of every high performer. It doesn't shout, but it always shows up.

Discipline is not glamorous, exciting, or Instagrammable, but it is powerful. It gets things done, moves the needle, builds trust with yourself, and makes you reliable—not just to others but to your own vision. That kind of integrity is magnetic. It's not about perfection: it's about repetition. Discipline compounds. The more you do it, the easier it becomes. Over time, what started as a sacrifice becomes second nature. What once required willpower now runs on rhythm.

Discipline is the rhythm of champions. Discipline is the delivery system of destiny. It's how you turn passion into purpose and dreams into daily action. It's the glue that binds desire and determination into legacy. When you combine these three forces—desire, determination, and discipline—you don't just move forward; you accelerate. You don't just reach goals; you exceed them. You don't just build success; you build substance. Together, desire, determination, and discipline form the engine of Focused Discipline. One without the others will burn out. Together, they create lasting momentum and meaningful results.

SUMMARY: CHAPTER SIX—KEY TAKEAWAYS

- Desire sparks the journey; it awakens purpose and sets goals in motion.

- Determination is the decision to keep going when desire wears thin.

- Discipline gives form and structure to desire and determination.

- You can't wait for desire; you must stir it through action and clarity.

- Motivation fades, but determination and discipline keep you moving.

- True desire aligns with purpose, not envy or pressure.

- Discipline creates consistency, and consistency compounds results.

- These three forces must work together for lasting success.

"Desire is the spark, determination is the fuel, and discipline is the engine that carries you to your destiny."

Desire and determination are partners. To harness them, schedule specific times for your most important tasks and guard them fiercely. Passion is powerful when channeled through structure.

CHAPTER 7

THE DISCIPLINE OF FOCUS

"You get what you focus on."
—UNKNOWN

THE POWER OF FOCUS

In today's world, distraction is more accessible than ever. Notifications ping every few seconds, demanding your attention. Emails pile up by the hour. News cycles never sleep. Social media scrolls endlessly, offering both inspiration and interruption. Opportunities—both real and counterfeit—present themselves at every turn, all vying for a slice of your mental bandwidth. The world is noisy, fast-paced, and impatient.

In this storm of stimuli, the most powerful asset you have is not your intelligence, your energy, or even your talent; it's your focus. Focus enables you to bring your whole self to what matters most. It serves as the invisible boundary that protects your progress and preserves your peace. It is the ability to ignore what is popular in order to pursue what is purposeful. Focus transforms energy into achievement. It separates the distracted from the disciplined, the busy from the effective, and the scattered from the strategic.

Focused people do not have more time; they simply give more attention to what counts. You can't do everything. You can do the right thing. Doing the right thing consistently produces greatness. Focus helps you cut through the noise and lock into your unique assignment. It prevents you from being stretched too thin or chasing every shiny object. It empowers you to go deeper instead of wider, to master your craft instead of dabbling in distraction.

This is where Focused Discipline becomes more than a concept: it becomes a lifestyle. Train your mind and heart to focus on the things that matter most, and you reclaim your time, peace, and power. Stop reacting and start leading. Stop chasing and start building. Focus enables you to make measurable progress in a noisy world—not by doing more, but by doing what matters with more intentionality.

FOCUS FILTERS OUT THE NOISE

Every day, choices bombard you. From the moment you wake up, your attention pulls in dozens of directions. Emails, calls, texts, advertisements, obligations, invitations—they all compete for your limited bandwidth. Not all of these things are bad; most are not aligned with your purpose. Saying *yes* to too many good things diminishes your capacity to say *yes* to the great things. This is why focus is not just helpful but essential.

It is the filter that helps you distinguish between what is merely attractive and what is truly aligned. The discipline of focus means learning to say *no* more often than you say *yes*. It's not just about protecting your time; it's about protecting your purpose. Every *yes* is a seed, and every seed grows into something. Sow your attention into distractions, and you'll reap stress and stagnation. Sow it into purpose, and you'll reap clarity, momentum, and results.

Focus isn't a refusal to engage with the world: it's a decision to engage with what matters most. It means choosing what matters over what's urgent, and what's eternal over what's trending. Focus allows you to sift through the clutter and commit to what truly moves the needle. It is the scalpel that carves out excellence from the noise of mediocrity. Focus gives your priorities a voice. It silences the voice of comparison, minimizes distractions, and protects your time.

It gives you permission to say, "This is not for me right now," without guilt. A focused life is a protected life. You begin to discern between good and best, between noise and necessity. You stop chasing everything and start building something. You go from wandering to working, from reacting to leading. Focus gives you clarity. Clarity gives you peace.

When you know what matters most, you stop being enslaved by what everyone else expects. You operate from a place of vision, not pressure. You build a life that is aligned, not scattered. One of the most powerful things you can do is conduct a focus audit. Look at how you're spending your time, where your energy is going, and what thoughts dominate your mind. Be brutally honest. Then ask, "Are these things helping me fulfill my purpose or pulling me away from it?"

You may find that some things you've labeled as important are really just urgent distractions. Others may be good opportunities, but not right for this season. Clarity leads to strategy, and strategy demands focus. When you are focused, you stop living by reaction and start living by design. You stop being owned by your schedule and start owning your schedule. Focus allows you to reclaim your life from the grip of busyness and aimless activity and realign with your God-given mission.

THE COST OF DISTRACTION

Distraction isn't just a delay: it's a detour. Sometimes, it's a destiny thief. It doesn't show up wearing a red warning label. It disguises itself as productivity, people-pleasing, and urgency. It looks like being busy, but it doesn't lead to a breakthrough. It feels like progress but produces pressure without purpose. The more distracted you are, the harder it is to hear your own thoughts, let alone the voice of God.

You can be pulled in a hundred directions and still never move forward. That's the silent danger of distraction. When you lose focus, you waste energy. You dilute impact. You trade depth for breadth. Instead of moving deeply in the direction of your calling, you skim the surface of many things without finishing any of them. You say *yes* to too many people, projects, and platforms, and in the process, you say *no* to the things that matter most.

Distraction scatters your attention, diffuses your strength, and undermines your effectiveness. It keeps you busy but barren, active but unfulfilled. Distraction comes in many forms: too many goals, too many commitments, too much screen time, too much comparison. It's not always the loud, obvious interruptions that rob your focus: it's the subtle drift caused by unchecked habits. It leaves you exhausted but empty, moving fast but going nowhere.

You can be running full speed in the wrong direction simply because you never stopped to focus. Even good things can become distractions when they're not aligned with your assignment. The discipline of focus requires awareness. You must recognize your distractions before you can remove them. Look honestly at the patterns that steal your time and the emotions that drive your behavior.

Are you procrastinating on what matters due to being overwhelmed by lesser tasks? Are you overcommitted out of fear of missing out or letting others down? These questions require courage and clarity. Ask yourself:

- What steals my attention most often?

- What activities make me feel busy but don't move me forward?

- Where do I need to set boundaries?

- What commitments do I need to renegotiate?

- Who or what is consuming my emotional energy without contributing to my growth?

Clarity is the antidote to distraction. But clarity doesn't happen by accident; it requires intention. Taking a step back, silencing the noise, and recalibrating your priorities is essential. Take time to reflect, pray, journal, and revisit your purpose often. Schedule time to disconnect from the noise of the world so you can reconnect with the voice of God.

Focus is fragile. It must be guarded not just occasionally but daily. Protect your focus like it's your future—in many ways, it is.

TRAINING YOUR FOCUS MUSCLE

Focus is not just a gift: it's a muscle. The more you use it, the stronger it gets;the less you use it, the weaker it becomes. Like any muscle, focus must be trained intentionally. Training your focus means creating rhythms that anchor your attention. It means designing your environment, calendar, and habits to support your vision.

Start your day with intentionality. Don't let the world set your agenda. Spend the first part of your morning in quiet reflection, prayer, and planning. Identify your top 1–3 priorities for the day—things that will actually move your life or work forward. Then commit to those priorities first.

Create focus blocks in your schedule; blocks of time where you do deep work. Turn off notifications. Set your phone on airplane mode if needed. Use tools like timers or accountability partners to stay on track. Remove the temptation to multitask. Discipline your mind to stay present. If your thoughts wander, bring them back. If your attention drifts, refocus. This mental discipline, like physical training, yields long-term strength. You are reconditioning your brain to prioritize depth over distraction.

BUILD HABITS THAT REINFORCE YOUR FOCUS:

- Keep a distraction list; write down ideas or impulses and revisit them later.

- Take short breaks to recharge.

- Use visual reminders of your goals.

- Reflect weekly on what's working and what needs adjustment.

Over time, these habits will sharpen your mental edge and make you more effective, more peaceful, and more purposeful.

THE SPIRITUAL SIDE OF FOCUS

Focus isn't just a productivity tool: it's a spiritual weapon. In a world where spiritual warfare is real, the enemy often uses distraction as one of his most effective tactics. When your heart is set on a divine assignment, the enemy will attack your focus before anything else. A distracted person cannot walk in dominion. They may still be moving, but not with purpose. They may still be working, but not with impact. Focused people are dangerous to darkness. They move with precision, authority, and intentionality. They are not easily swayed by pressure, comparison, or fatigue; they are anchored in purpose.

That's why Scripture often speaks of setting your heart, fixing your eyes, and renewing your mind. Focus is not only a mindset: it's an act of worship. It's an intentional decision to devote your energy to the One who gave you your assignment. God honors focus because it reflects devotion and communicates trust. Jesus lived with focused discipline; He said, "I must be about My Father's business." He didn't try to do everything. He focused on the assignment and said *no* to distractions, even good ones, to say *yes* to God's perfect plan.

In Proverbs 4:25–27, we're instructed: "Let your eyes look straight ahead; fix your gaze directly before you. Give careful thought to the paths for your feet... Do not turn to the right or the left; keep your foot from evil." This isn't just poetic wisdom: it's a blueprint for strategic living. When your eyes are fixed, your path becomes clear. When your gaze is steady, your feet avoid compromise. Focus guards your heart from double-mindedness and your life from detours.

As believers, our focus must be rooted in purpose and sharpened by discipline. This kind of focus doesn't come naturally, but through intentional surrender. It is cultivated through prayer, reflection, and spiritual maturity. When your focus is clear, your path is stable. When your path is stable, your progress becomes undeniable. You won't be blown by the winds of culture, confusion, or convenience; you will walk in clarity, confidence, and calling. Spiritual focus also keeps you anchored when the world is shifting. You're not swayed by every trend or tossed by every trial. You move with divine direction, knowing that God orders the steps of the focused and faithful. You understand that time is a gift, not a guarantee. You don't just want to be successful; you want to be surrendered. That kind of focus is not just powerful: it's unstoppable.

REALIGNING WHEN YOU DRIFT

Even the most disciplined people lose focus at times. Life happens. Emotions fluctuate. Emergencies arise. Seasons shift. What once felt clear can become clouded by busyness, fatigue, or emotional weariness. The key is not to beat yourself up: it's to realign quickly. Drift happens when we don't recalibrate, and the longer we drift, the harder it is to regain momentum. Focus is not a permanent state, but a daily decision. It must be maintained, renewed, and occasionally reestablished. That's why awareness and humility are critical. You have to be willing to pause, assess, and adjust.

Focus is like a compass: when it starts to point in the wrong direction, you don't panic. You simply correct the course and keep moving. Take time regularly to reflect: Am I still focused on what matters most? Has something crept into my schedule or mindset that needs to be released? What boundaries need to be reinforced? Where have I compromised clarity for convenience? These are not signs of failure but of maturity. Maturity recognizes that staying on course requires constant course correction.

Sometimes, regaining focus is as simple as unplugging. A few hours offline, a walk in silence, a conversation with a mentor, a time of worship or journaling, or a moment of stillness with God can help. These recalibration points restore your spiritual alignment and mental clarity. They help you listen to what your heart has been trying to say beneath the noise of obligation. You don't need to start over; you just need to return to your why, reset your targets, and reengage your discipline. Like a plane making minor adjustments to stay on course, you can realign and regain momentum without abandoning the journey. Realignment isn't regression: it's restoration. It brings your energy, intention, and vision back into agreement with your purpose.

THE RESULTS OF FOCUSED LIVING

When you master the discipline of focus, everything improves. You get more done in less time, not by rushing or multitasking, but by channeling your attention into high-impact actions. You become a better steward of your time, your energy, and your thoughts. Each hour becomes intentional. Each task is connected to a bigger purpose. Focus multiplies your efforts. You experience deeper fulfillment because you are no longer scattered across a dozen half-finished goals. Instead, you are moving steadily in the direction of what truly matters. There is peace in knowing that your time and talent are being invested in something meaningful.

Focus brings alignment between who you are and what you do; alignment breeds joy. You create margin for rest and creativity. When your schedule is not overcrowded with distraction, you make room for renewal. You find space to think, reflect, and hear from God. You begin to dream again. Focus doesn't just make you efficient: it makes you whole. You become more present in your relationships. When your mind is not cluttered, your heart is available. You can show up fully for your spouse, your children, your friends, and your team. You listen better. You love better. You lead better. Focus deepens connection.

You stop surviving and start advancing. Focused people don't just wait for life to happen: they build it. They don't just maintain but multiply. They don't just drift but direct. Every step becomes intentional. Every decision is rooted in vision. Focus transforms your pace, your path, and your potential. Focus leads to mastery. It allows you to go deep instead of staying shallow. It transforms scattered effort into strategic results. When you are focused, you're not chasing a hundred things halfway: you're pursuing one thing wholeheartedly. Mastery is never a product of distraction: it is always the fruit of devotion.

SUMMARY: CHAPTER SEVEN—KEY TAKEAWAYS

- Focus is your most powerful asset in a noisy, distracted world.

- Discipline helps you say *no* to distraction so you can say *yes* to purpose.

- Distraction is a destiny thief; guard your attention fiercely.

- Focus is a muscle; train it daily through rhythms, routines, and boundaries.

- Clarity is the antidote to distraction; revisit your goals and priorities often.

- Spiritual focus keeps you aligned with your divine assignment and grounded in peace.

- Realign quickly when you drift; refocus, reset, and move forward with grace.

- The fruit of focus is fulfillment, mastery, and measurable progress.

"You don't need more time; you need more focus."

CHAPTER 8

THE HABIT OF SHOWING UP

"Eighty percent of success is showing up."
—WOODY ALLEN

CONSISTENCY OVER INTENSITY

Consistency beats intensity every time. While the world celebrates overnight success, real growth usually results from daily decisions made faithfully over time. It's not the big, loud moments that build your future: it's the quiet, consistent ones. It's the habit of showing up. Focused Discipline thrives on this habit. In every field—business, fitness, faith, family—the people who show up daily are the ones who move forward. Not because they're the smartest or the most inspired, but because they're committed. Commitment closes the gap between goals and growth.

Showing up doesn't always look glamorous. Sometimes it's early mornings, late nights, and in-between moments. Sometimes it's doing what needs to be done when no one is watching. Sometimes it's choosing faithfulness when you feel frustrated or progress when you feel stuck. But showing up is never wasted. It builds muscle, memory, and momentum. Over time, this rhythm of presence becomes the foundation of breakthrough. You don't rise to the level of your potential: you rise to the level of your habits. The habit of showing up positions you for impact.

THE MYTH OF MOTIVATION

One of the biggest lies of our generation is that you need to feel inspired to act. Discipline doesn't wait for motivation; it creates it. When you show up consistently, regardless of your mood, you train your mind to follow your mission instead of your emotions. That, over time, creates a stronger, more stable version of you. Motivation is fleeting. It comes and goes. It depends on mood, circumstances, and environment. Discipline is stable. It shows up even when you don't feel like it. Discipline wakes you up when the alarm rings. It helps you say *no* when temptation whispers. It keeps your word when no one's watching. Discipline moves your life forward, inch by inch, step by step.

Let's break down the core myths people believe about motivation:

1. "I have to feel it to do it."

The truth is, feelings are unreliable indicators for action. If you only act when you feel like it, you'll rarely build momentum. High performers understand that action leads to feeling, not the other way around.

2. "Motivation comes from the outside."

Motivation can be sparked by a great message or a crisis; however, long-term motivation must come from within. It is fueled by vision, purpose, and internal clarity. If you depend on others to hype you up, you'll burn out when applause fades.

3. "Discipline is harsh and robotic."

On the contrary, discipline is freeing. It eliminates decision fatigue. It gives structure to your goals. It produces long-term peace. Discipline makes space for creativity, joy, and fulfillment to flourish.

4. "Motivated people are born that way."

No one is born consistent: they train for it. Every disciplined person you admire built that strength through daily choices. Motivation is not a personality trait but a pattern of response.

5. "Once I'm motivated, I'll follow through."

The reverse is true. Follow-through produces motivation. Every time you complete a small task, your brain receives a reward signal that reinforces behavior. Motivation is a byproduct of momentum.

Motivation may get you started, but only discipline keeps you going. The habit of showing up makes your actions less dependent on mood and more connected to mission. You don't always feel like it. You do it anyway. Growth lives on the other side of obedience. This mindset separates the dreamers from the doers. The dreamer says, "I'll wait until I'm ready." The doer says, "I'll start now and grow into the readiness." Every step you take, even when uninspired, is a seed sown into your future. The harvest always comes.

WHY CONSISTENCY WINS

The most successful people aren't always the most brilliant, but they are the most consistent. They don't just work hard when it's convenient. They work smart when it counts. They know that trust is built over time, and excellence is forged through repetition. They understand the compound effect: small, repeated actions create massive long-term impact.

Consistency creates reliability. It tells your mind, your body, and your world that you can be trusted. Trust builds confidence. Confidence builds momentum. Momentum builds results. Every time you show up—on time, in position, with the right mindset—you're investing in your future self. You're casting a vote for who you're becoming. You're building trust with yourself; over time, that trust becomes confidence. That confidence becomes capacity, and that capacity becomes character. Small disciplines, repeated daily, lead to giant results. You don't have to sprint every day: you just need to keep moving. Some days you'll feel like running. Other days, all you can manage is a slow walk. That's okay. The goal is not to be perfect: it's to be present.

Consistency wins because it builds internal credibility. When you know that you show up for yourself, your self-respect grows. Your mental toughness strengthens. You begin to believe in your word, in your will, and in your ability to follow through.

THE FAITHFULNESS FACTOR

Faithfulness is not just a spiritual word but a leadership strategy. Scripture says, "He who is faithful with little will be faithful with much." Why? Showing up when it's small proves that you can be trusted when it grows. The habit of faithfulness is one of the clearest indicators of future success. Don't despise the days of small beginnings. The habit of showing up is how you grow from hidden to honored, from overlooked to undeniable. It's how you build the kind of life—and legacy—that stands the test of time.

Some of the most successful people in history didn't start with applause: they started with obscurity. They served faithfully in the shadows. They showed up when it wasn't glamorous. Because they were faithful in private, they were prepared for visibility. Faithfulness is not about perfection but presence. It's not about being the loudest: it's about being the most grounded. You keep showing up in prayer. You keep tending to your assignment even when it seems insignificant. Faithfulness is never wasted in the kingdom of God. Even when it doesn't feel like it's working, keep showing up. Even when no one notices, keep showing up. Even when your pace is slow, keep showing up. Even when you're discouraged, keep showing up. What you repeat, you reinforce. What you reinforce, you become.

Showing up is how seeds are watered. It's how skills are sharpened. It's how doors begin to open. Don't underestimate the power of presence. Showing up is proof that you still believe.

HARRIS D. McFARLARE

SHOWING UP IN DIFFERENT SEASONS

There are seasons when showing up looks different. In times of grief, it may be just getting out of bed and taking a deep breath. It may be simply praying when the words don't come easily. In seasons of waiting, showing up may look like continuing to learn, to plan, or to serve faithfully while nothing around you seems to be changing. In moments of transition, it may mean saying *yes* to new responsibilities with uncertainty and courage.

Showing up doesn't always mean high performance. Sometimes it just means presence. Sometimes it means endurance. Sometimes it means doing the next right thing. In seasons of loss, showing up might look like being kind to yourself. Giving yourself grace. Not quitting when your emotions are raw and your heart feels numb. Even just doing the basics—eating, praying, resting—can be powerful acts of resilience.

In times of spiritual dryness, showing up may mean simply opening your Bible, attending church, or whispering a prayer when your soul feels empty. In high-pressure seasons, showing up could mean prioritizing rest and drawing healthy boundaries so that your *yes* remains meaningful. In every season, presence is powerful. It signals to heaven and to your own soul that you haven't given up. That you're still invested. That you still believe there is purpose in the process. You're still in the game.

You're still moving. You're still expecting something good. Even if your steps are small, they matter. Showing up keeps your heart engaged even when your hands are tired. It honors God. It strengthens your inner resolve. It prepares you for what's next.

You don't always get to control the season, but you can always control your presence in it. Consistency keeps your spirit rooted when circumstances are shifting. It keeps your values anchored when emotions are volatile. Showing up when it's inconvenient trains your character. Showing up when it's uncomfortable develops your strength. Ask any athlete, artist, or entrepreneur—success didn't come overnight. It came through the grind. Through repetition. Through the silent, unseen moments. Through the daily discipline of showing up.

When you're consistent through the hard times, you'll be ready when opportunity knocks. You won't need to scramble or strive; you'll already be in position.

SHOWING UP FOR OTHERS

The habit of showing up isn't just about your own goals; it's also about the people you're called to impact. Your presence can be a gift to others. When you consistently show up for your team, your spouse, your children, your clients, and your community, you create trust and influence. Leaders who show up are leaders people trust.

Friends who show up are friends who are remembered. Spouses who show up build marriages that last. Parents who show up raise confident children.

It's not always about having the right words; it's about being there. Your showing up says, "You matter." It says, "I'm committed." It says, "We're in this together." In a world where flakiness and self-centeredness have become normal, a consistent presence is revolutionary.

FROM EFFORT TO IDENTITY

The more you show up, the more you realize—it's not just about what you're doing. It's about who you're becoming. The habit of showing up reshapes your identity. You stop seeing yourself as inconsistent, unreliable, or unsure. You begin to see yourself as someone who is focused, disciplined, and dependable. Identity change doesn't happen overnight. It happens through repetition. Every time you show up, you reinforce a new narrative: "I'm not who I used to be. I'm growing. I'm building. I'm becoming." Over time, the habit becomes second nature.

You stop negotiating with excuses. You stop questioning your worth. You wake up and move forward—not because it's easy, but because it's who you are.

SUMMARY: CHAPTER EIGHT—KEY TAKEAWAYS

- Showing up consistently is more powerful than waiting for inspiration.

- Daily faithfulness beats random bursts of intensity.

- Consistency builds trust, confidence, and capacity.

- Discipline creates momentum, even when motivation is low.

- The habit of showing up is how you build the life you want.

- Faithfulness in obscurity prepares you for visibility.

- Your presence in every season matters, whether progress is visible or not.

- Showing up for others builds trust, relationships, and influence.

- Repetition reshapes identity. Discipline rewrites your future.

"Success doesn't come from what you do occasionally. It comes from what you do consistently."

Showing up consistently turns intentions into results. Identify an area where you have been sporadic and commit to a simple, repeatable action each day. Consistency compounds.

CHAPTER 9

THE POWER OF FOLLOW-THROUGH

"It's not just about starting; it's about finishing."
—UNKNOWN

It's one thing to start; it's another thing to finish. Beginnings are exciting, carrying a sense of novelty and inspiration. A new vision, a fresh idea, or a compelling goal can ignite passion in almost anyone. Starting feels powerful, promising possibility.

THE IMPORTANCE OF FINISHING

If starting is the spark, finishing is the fire that sustains the vision until it becomes reality. Fire takes fuel: discipline, resilience, and relentless focus. Ideas are common. Excitement is easy. Follow-through? That's rare.

Follow-through separates wishful thinkers from actual achievers. It's where theory becomes transformation. It's where effort becomes evidence. It's where potential becomes progress. It's where Focused Discipline proves its worth, not in how well you begin, but in how well you continue and complete. Real success isn't born in the rush of a new beginning; it's forged in the steady rhythm of sustained action.

THE CHALLENGE OF FOLLOW-THROUGH

Everyone has intentions. Few have follow-through. The difference between the two often determines success or stagnation, impact or inconsistency, growth or frustration. Most people start with excitement but stop when things get hard, boring, or uncomfortable. They pivot at the first sign of pressure. Those who commit to follow-through, even despite delay, distraction, or difficulty, become the people who build something that lasts.

FOLLOW-THROUGH AS A SECRET WEAPON

In a world constantly distracted by what's next, follow-through is a secret weapon. It makes your word matter, your goals real, and your vision credible. When you consistently follow through, people know they can depend on you. Your commitments carry weight.

Your goals gain traction. Your life builds substance. Leadership begins to inspire not because of flashy beginnings, but because of faithful completions.

STARTING IS EMOTIONAL. FINISHING IS INTENTIONAL.

Let's face it: starting is fun. It's filled with possibilities. Energy is high. Motivation is fresh. You feel invincible, fueled by vision and hope. You imagine the end from the beginning, dreaming of outcomes and rewards. Starting feels like momentum, like progress, like destiny in motion. That emotional rush at the beginning of any new journey is real and powerful.

THE MESSY MIDDLE

When the honeymoon phase ends, reality kicks in. The schedule tightens. Distractions creep in. The grind begins. Feelings fade. The vision becomes blurry. It's here in the messy middle that most people abandon what they once committed to. This occurs not due to a lack of worthiness, but because it's no longer exciting. The silence after the spark separates the committed from the casual. This is where Focused Discipline steps in.

THE ROLE OF DISCIPLINE

When emotion evaporates, discipline remains. Focus sustains you when passion is no longer loud. Discipline carries you when motivation has gone quiet. This is where maturity takes over. You stop chasing the feeling and start honoring the assignment. Finishing requires intention. It means continuing when excitement runs dry. It means pushing through resistance, boredom, obstacles, and delays. You honor the vision not for the good feelings it brings, but because it still matters. You keep showing up, not for applause, but for alignment. You finish not because it's easy, but because it's yours to finish.

THE MASTERY OF FOLLOW-THROUGH

Anyone can make a resolution. Anyone can launch a business, start a book, join a gym, or plan a project. The ones who finish, who actually see it through, master follow-through. That mastery is not built on hype; it's built on habit. Step by step. Bit by bit. Word by word. It's found in the moments where you push past excuses and press into excellence. The emotional high of beginning something new must give way to the daily discipline of continuing when no one is clapping. The real power lies in the quiet resolve that says, "I will see this through."

That resolve is the seed of greatness. It's not flashy. It's not loud. It's faithful. Faithful finishers always leave a mark.

WHY FOLLOW-THROUGH BUILDS CREDIBILITY

Follow-through is how you build trust, both with others and with yourself. Every time you follow through, you reinforce the message: "I'm dependable. I do what I say. I finish what I start." When you don't follow through, you train yourself to expect inconsistency. Over time, you begin to doubt your own ability to execute. Your confidence shrinks. Your belief in your own word weakens. Your motivation becomes hollow. This is why many people feel stuck; it's not that they don't have goals. It's that they no longer trust themselves to achieve them. Repeated self-betrayal breaks inner credibility.

THE GOOD NEWS

Here's the good news: follow-through is a skill. It can be developed. You can rebuild trust inyourself. You can grow in consistency. As you do, your sense of confidence and clarity will return stronger than ever. People around you take notice, too. In business, consistent follow-through builds your reputation. In relationships, it deepens connection. In leadership, it earns respect. Others begin to believe in your vision as they've seen your consistency.

THE ENEMIES OF FOLLOW-THROUGH

To master follow-through, you need to understand what gets in the way. These aren't just obstacles; they are patterns of thinking and behavior that subtly sabotage progress. Identifying them is the first step to replacing them with discipline and direction. Here are five common enemies that sabotage consistency:

1. Over-committing

One of the most common reasons people fail to follow through is that they try to do too much at once. Ambition is good, but when it lacks focus, it becomes a liability. Spreading yourself too thin causes you to start many things but finish few. Follow-through thrives on simplicity. When your plate is too full, everything suffers. The key is to prioritize. Say *yes* to the most important, most aligned goals; learn to say *no* to the rest. Choose fewer things and do them better.

2. Perfectionism

Perfectionism disguises itself as excellence; it's really fear in a tuxedo. The fear of not getting it right keeps people from ever finishing. They tinker endlessly, revise obsessively, and delay action indefinitely, all in the name of getting it perfect. Perfection is a moving target. What matters more is momentum. Excellence is important, but it must be balanced with execution. Done is better than perfect. Finished is better than flawless. Give your best; don't let the quest for perfection rob you of the satisfaction of progress.

3. Procrastination

Procrastination is the silent killer of dreams. It whispers that you can do it later, and later becomes never. It hides behind distractions and false urgency, creating a constant undercurrent of guilt and stress. Procrastination isn't a time problem; it's a focus problem. The solution is to break large tasks into manageable parts and take action daily, even if it's small. Discipline erodes delay. When you build momentum, procrastination loses its grip. Show up before you feel ready. Progress breeds clarity.

6. Lack of Clarity

You can't finish what you haven't clearly defined. When your goals are vague, your follow-through will be weak. Lack of clarity leads to confusion, frustration, and ultimately disengagement. Clarity is power. You must define success in measurable, attainable terms. What does "done" look like? What does progress feel like?

Create a clear target so you can focus your energy with precision. Clarity simplifies decision-making and fuels commitment.

4. Emotional Fatigue

Emotional exhaustion can make even simple tasks feel overwhelming. When your tank is empty, follow-through becomes a burden rather than a commitment. Fatigue often comes from constant decision-making, unspoken pressure, or burnout from trying to prove yourself. That's why rest is not a reward; it's a requirement. Reconnect with your vision. Recenter your mind through prayer, solitude, journaling, or meaningful conversations. Protect your peace. You can't finish strong if you're running on empty.

The more you recognize these patterns, the more power you have to overcome them. Awareness gives you choice; intentional action is the path forward. Eliminate these enemies, and your capacity to follow through will multiply.

SMALL FINISHES CREATE BIG MOMENTUM

We often think of follow-through in terms of big wins: launching a business, finishing a book, or running a marathon. The real magic of follow-through lives in the small things.

- Finishing the workout.
- Sending the email you've been avoiding.
- Making the uncomfortable phone call.
- Following up with a client.
- Praying every morning.
- Sticking to your budget for one more week.

Each Vote for Your Identity

Each of these is a vote for your identity. Each one builds momentum. Each one strengthens your follow-through muscle. Momentum results from completion. When you finish a task—no matter how small—your brain releases a hit of dopamine. That reward builds confidence and motivation. Over time, it creates a new pattern in your brain: I finish what I start. Do not wait for the big moment. Start with what's in front of you. Finish the small things. Celebrate the wins. They're not minor; they're momentum-builders.

FAITH, VISION, AND FINISHING WELL

Scripture is full of references to perseverance and finishing. Paul said, "I have fought the good fight, I have finished the race, I have kept the faith." (2 Timothy 4:7). Jesus Himself declared from the cross, "It is finished." These are not just words of conclusion;

they are declarations of destiny fulfilled. They reflect lives that refused to quit, missions completed with integrity, and callings honored to the end. God values finishers. Throughout the Bible, those who endure are commended, not merely those who begin. Faithfulness to the end is a repeated theme, as it reflects God's own nature. He is the Author and the Finisher. He does not abandon what He starts; as His children, we're called to mirror that same spirit of perseverance.

In the kingdom, follow-through is not just about productivity; it's about faithfulness. It's not about how much you achieve in the eyes of man, but how faithful you are to what God has asked you to steward. When you say *yes* to an assignment from heaven, you accept more than a goal; you accept a divine trust. When you start something under God's direction, you commit not only to a goal but to a stewardship. You become responsible for what has been entrusted to you. That business, that ministry, that book, that calling; it's not just your dream. It's your assignment. Every assignment carries weight, purpose, and accountability. Assignments deserve your follow-through.

THE IMPACT OF FOLLOW-THROUGH

Why? Every time you finish what God gave you to start, heaven rejoices while hell loses ground. You become a living testimony that the Word works, that faith endures, and that vision can be trusted. Every step toward the finish line is a declaration of victory over the temptation to quit. This means you don't just push through for your own benefit. You follow through to honor the One who gave you the vision. It reflects His character; God is a finisher. He completes what He starts, fulfills every promise, and empowers us to do the same. We carry the baton with grace, run our race with endurance, and leave no word unfinished and no calling unfulfilled.

Faith-filled follow-through means trusting God even when progress seems slow. It means staying the course even when results aren't visible, obeying even when others don't understand, continuing to write when no one is reading, continuing to serve when no one says thank you, and continuing to believe when the fruit hasn't yet appeared. This is Focused Discipline at its highest form; faithfully finishing what God has begun in you. Finishing well is a legacy. Your legacy isn't just what you accomplish; it's what you complete. It's the story that says, "They didn't just start strong. They stayed strong. They finished in faith."

FOCUSED DISCIPLINE

WHAT FINISHING LOOKS LIKE PRACTICALLY

To build the habit of follow-through, you need a system that works in real life. Here are six keys to finishing well:

1. Set a clear finish line

Define what "done" looks like. Vague goals lead to vague execution. Write your finish line in a way that can be measured.

2. Schedule Time to Work on It

If it doesn't have a place in your calendar, it won't get done. Don't wait for free time; make time. Block it out. Protect it.

3. Break It Down

Big goals need bite-sized steps. What can you finish today that moves you forward? Create checkpoints along the way.

4. Track Your Progress

Progress is motivating. Keep a journal, checklist, or tracker. Seeing growth keeps you engaged and focused.

5. Set Reminders of Your "Why"

When motivation dips, your reason will carry you. Keep

your vision visible; on your wall, in your journal, or as a daily affirmation.

6. Finish Even When It's Messy

Don't give up because it got hard. Don't wait for perfect conditions. Finish anyway. You can revise. You can refine. Finish first.

Following through becomes easier when it becomes part of your identity. Tell yourself daily, "I am a finisher." Prove it by doing what you said you would do.

THE DISCIPLINE OF COMPLETION

Completion is a discipline. It's not about speed; it's about sustainability. When you build a habit of finishing what you start, you create a standard for your life. You begin to attract opportunities, relationships, and responsibilities that match your level of follow-through. You also inspire others. People follow leaders who finish. People respect those who deliver. Your family, your team, and your audience don't just hear your words—they watch your consistency.

Completion also liberates mental space. Open loops—unfinished tasks and unresolved goals—create anxiety and clutter. Finishing clears the clutter. It frees your focus. It gives you peace. When you become a finisher, you walk lighter. You speak with more authority. You live with deeper fulfillment. Completion is not about crossing a line; it's about becoming the kind of person who does what they commit to.

WHEN TO LET GO (AND WHEN TO PUSH THROUGH)

Sometimes, not finishing is actually the right decision. There's a difference between quitting out of frustration and releasing something that no longer aligns with your assignment. Here's how you discern the difference:

- **Push through if** it's hard yet still aligned with your purpose. If the resistance is part of your growth, stay the course.

- **Let go if** the goal is no longer true to your calling. If it was birthed in comparison, fear, or pride, release it with wisdom and grace.

FOLLOW-THROUGH: STEWARDSHIP OVER STUBBORNNESS

Follow-through is not about stubbornness; it's about stewardship. Know what God has called you to finish. Let go of the rest. The right finish isn't just about reaching the end; it's about finishing the right thing, in the right spirit, for the right reason.

SUMMARY: CHAPTER NINE—KEY TAKEAWAYS

- Starting is emotional; finishing is intentional.

- Follow-through builds self-trust and personal credibility.

- The enemies of follow-through include over commitment, perfectionism, procrastination, lack of clarity, and emotional fatigue.

- Small completions create massive momentum.

- Faithfulness to God includes finishing your assignment.

- Completion is a form of mental and spiritual clarity.

- Discern what is worth finishing and what needs releasing.

- Progress is found not in hype; progress lies in habit.

"Anyone can start strong. The power is in finishing well."

CHAPTER 10

THE POWER OF SAYING NO

"The difference between successful people and really successful people is that really successful people say no to almost everything."
—WARREN BUFFETT

THE POWER OF SAYING NO

In a world that constantly demands more—more time, more attention, more involvement—one of the most powerful tools for staying focused is the ability to say *no*. We live in a culture that celebrates hustle, applauds busyness, and equates saying *yes* with ambition and openness. Too many yeses can lead to exhaustion, frustration, and fragmentation. Focused Discipline requires more than doing a lot; it requires doing the right things with clarity, purpose, and consistency. That starts with learning how and when to say *no*.

Not all yeses are created equal. Some will push you closer to your purpose. Others will simply maintain your current pace. Some will pull you completely off track. The difference isn't always obvious; however, the impact is undeniable. A misaligned yes can divert your energy, dilute your focus, and derail your destiny. That's why saying *no* is not just a leadership skill; it's a life-preserving discipline. Discipline isn't just about what you commit to; it's also about what you have the wisdom and courage to decline.

Saying *no* is not about selfishness; it's about stewardship. It means you understand that your time, your energy, your influence, and your relationships are sacred resources. To protect what matters most, you must learn to reject what doesn't. Every time you say *yes* to something, you are by default saying *no* to something else. There's always a trade-off. Saying *yes* to every meeting might mean saying *no* to quality time with your family. Accepting every social event might mean declining personal rest and reflection. Agreeing to every project might mean sacrificing excellence in your core assignment.

THE IMPORTANCE OF DISCERNMENT

That's why Focused Discipline demands discernment. Without boundaries, you'll become busy yet ineffective, present yet unproductive, active yet not aligned. You might gain approval, yet you'll lose peace. You might be included, yet not fulfilled. With clarity and courage, your *no* becomes a gate that protects your mission and your mental health. It becomes a filter that keeps distractions out and lets purpose flow freely. A disciplined *no* makes room for a powerful *yes*: the *yes* to purpose, the *yes* to calling, and the *yes* to the life you were designed to live.

WHY SAYING NO IS SO HARD

Let's be honest; saying *no* is uncomfortable, especially if you're kind, capable, or driven. You don't want to disappoint others. You don't want to miss out. You don't want to seem ungrateful or uninterested. There's a social pressure to be agreeable, to be available, and to appear accommodating, even when it comes at your own expense. Trying to please everyone is a fast track to burnout and broken focus. You can't fulfill your purpose while constantly managing everyone else's expectations. People-pleasing is not leadership. It is certainly not discipline. It's compromise disguised as kindness.

What looks like generosity on the outside can become resentment on the inside when you continually say yes to avoid discomfort. Saying *no* doesn't mean you're harsh. It means you're honest. It means you've counted the cost and have chosen to steward your time, energy, and attention intentionally. It means you're more committed to your mission than to momentary approval. It shows maturity and wisdom because not everything is meant for you; even if it looks good, feels flattering, or appears urgent.

Saying *no* is often hardest when the request involves people you love, respect, or serve. You want to be helpful. You want to contribute. You want to show that you care. Remember this: when you say *yes* to everyone else's priorities, you often say *no* to your own. You spread yourself thin, eventually breaking your own rhythm, compromising your boundaries, and jeopardizing your focus.

Most people struggle with saying *no*; they haven't defined their *yes*. When your priorities are vague, everything feels equally important. Everything seems urgent. Everything appears deserving. Once your purpose is clear, your *no* becomes clear too. A defined *yes* empowers a confident *no*. It gives you the framework to evaluate every request: Does this align with my purpose? Will this move me closer to my vision? Is this part of what I'm called to do right now? When your *yes* is anchored in clarity, your *no* doesn't feel like rejection; it feels like direction.

THE COST OF EVERY YES

Your time, energy, and attention are not infinite. They are precious, non-renewable resources that must be managed with discernment. Every *yes* you speak carries an invisible cost, whether you see it immediately or not. It costs time you won't get back. It costs energy you can't invest elsewhere. It costs focus that could have been directed toward what truly matters most. Every commitment requires capacity. Every opportunity consumes something.

You may be able to do a lot, but you cannot do it all and do it well. When you continue saying *yes* without limits, you eventually begin to compromise your health, your excellence, your peace, or your relationships. Something always pays for an unguarded *yes*. When you say *yes* out of obligation rather than alignment, you're sacrificing impact. It might feel noble in the moment; however, over time, it leads to depletion. When you say *yes* to what's urgent over what's essential, you're not managing your time; you're surrendering it. You become reactive rather than proactive.

When you say *yes* to too many people, you say *no* to the depth of your own assignment. You trade intimacy for spread, depth for breadth, and meaning for motion. Every *yes* should pass through a filter of purpose. Does this support my calling? Does it align with my values? Does it make room for rest and renewal? Saying *yes* to everything is not generosity; it's unsustainable. Often, it's rooted in fear: fear of letting people down, fear of missing out, fear of being seen as unavailable or uncooperative.

Discipline says, "Not every door is my door." It means resisting distraction in the name of direction. It means learning to be okay with not being everywhere, doing everything, or pleasing everyone. In fact, Focused Discipline trains you to be more selective, not less available. The more focused you are, the more powerful your *yes* becomes; it's been sharpened by wisdom and guarded by intentionality.

STRATEGIC NO'S CREATE POWERFUL YESES

The most effective leaders are not those who do the most. They are those who do the most meaningful things with precision. They guard their *yes* like treasure. A well-placed *no* creates margin for what really matters, and a strategic *no* creates room for mastery. You can't master your craft if your schedule is crowded with distractions.

1. Protect Your Priorities

Your most important relationships and responsibilities deserve your best, not your leftovers.

2. Preserve Your Peace

Constant engagement leads to emotional depletion. Saying *no* maintains inner stability.

3. Fuel Your Focus

Every unnecessary commitment you release gives you energy to go deeper into what matters.

4. Reinforce Your Identity

Every *no* reminds you of who you are and what you're about. It keeps you grounded in your mission.

5. Strengthen Your Influence

People respect those who value their time. When your *yes* carries weight, others take it seriously.

6. Empower Your Team

Saying *no* gives others permission to step up. It decentralizes dependency and strengthens collaboration.

7. Promote Healthy Boundaries

You model what it means to lead without burnout. Your boundaries give others courage to do the same.

8. Create Space for Divine Interruption

When your schedule isn't maxed out, God has room to lead you spontaneously.

9. Train Your Discernment

With every no, you grow more skilled at filtering what aligns and what distracts.

A well-placed *no* is not a rejection; it's a declaration. It says, "I know who I am. I know what I'm called to. I won't dilute that by saying *yes* to everything."

HOW TO SAY NO WITH GRACE

You can say *no* without being rude. Discipline doesn't require arrogance; it requires boundaries. Here are some practical ways to say *no* gracefully:

1. Be clear and direct.

"Thank you for thinking of me; I'm not able to commit to that right now."

2. Honor the request.

"I really appreciate the opportunity; my focus is currently elsewhere."

3. Offer an alternative.

"I'm not available to help; however, I know someone who might be a good fit."

4. **Protect your time unapologetically.**

"I'm reserving this season for rest, reflection, and deep work."

5. **Don't over-explain.**

A simple, kind *no* is often more powerful than a defensive one.

BOUNDARIES DON'T NEED JUSTIFICATION

If the opportunity or request doesn't align with your goals, peace, or purpose, a polite *no* suffices.

SAYING NO TO GOOD TO SAY YES TO GREAT

One of the greatest tests of Focused Discipline lies not in saying *no* to bad things; it's in saying *no* to good things. The good is often more deceptive than the obviously wrong. It looks beneficial. It looks promising. It may even feel productive, yet good can be the enemy of the great if it diverts you from your God-ordained assignment. Sometimes, opportunities that come your way are attractive, exciting, and even beneficial. They align with your skill set and may even bring applause or affirmation.

The question isn't, "Is this good?" It's, "Is this aligned?" Good things are not always God things. What benefits someone else might become a burden to you if it pulls you away from your core purpose. Good things can still be the wrong fit. They can become distractions if they stretch your time too thin or dilute your energy from where it matters most. What starts as a noble intention can quietly become a subtle detour. When your life fills with good-but-misaligned yeses, you slowly lose your effectiveness in the one thing that truly matters.

Jesus modeled this perfectly. He didn't heal every person. He didn't visit every town. He didn't respond to every cry for attention. Instead, He stayed on mission. He said *no* to distraction, even when it came in the form of good intention, so He could say *yes* to the cross. He refused to be driven by people's demands. Instead, He followed divine direction. That's Focused Discipline in its purest form.

As your influence grows, so will your opportunities. People will want your time, your talent, your input. Invitations will increase. Requests will multiply. Not every open door is from God. Not every invitation is divine. Not every opportunity is yours to steward. That's why you need the wisdom to discern and the strength to decline. Discernment allows you to see beneath the surface. Strength gives you the courage to obey your boundaries.

It may hurt to say *no* to something good. It may even offend others. Remind yourself: you are not here to do everything; you are here to do what matters. Doing what matters requires the power to say *no* with clarity, confidence, and conviction.

NO IS A BOUNDARY, NOT A REJECTION

People may not always understand your *no*. That's okay. You are not called to manage everyone's expectations. You are called to manage your assignment. *No* is not rejection; it's redirection. It helps others adjust their expectations and find the right person for the right need. When you say *no* with clarity and kindness, you create trust. People learn that your *yes* means something, and your *no* is not personal.

Boundaries are healthy. They make relationships stronger. They prevent resentment. They communicate value. You are not serving others well when your *yes* comes from guilt, fear, or fatigue. You serve best when your *yes* comes from a place of clarity, energy, and purpose. That kind of *yes* is only possible when you've learned to say *no*.

FOCUSED DISCIPLINE

THE SPIRITUAL SIDE OF NO

Saying *no* is not just practical; it's deeply spiritual. It's an act of trust. It says, "I don't have to do everything to fulfill my calling. I trust God to open the right doors and close the wrong ones." Sometimes we say *yes* out of fear: fear of missing out, fear of being disliked, fear of losing relevance. God never calls us to make decisions from fear. He calls us to walk in wisdom and peace. Isaiah 30:21 says, "Your ears shall hear a word behind you, saying, 'This is the way, walk in it,' whenever you turn to the right hand or whenever you turn to the left." That means God is guiding you. You don't have to guess. You don't have to say *yes* to everything just to stay busy or look spiritual.

Jesus often withdrew to pray. He left crowds waiting. He walked away from urgent voices. Why? He was more interested in alignment than applause. If the Savior could say *no* to some things, so can we.

PRACTICE THE DISCIPLINE OF DISCERNMENT

Not every battle is yours. Not every assignment is forever. Not every opportunity is meant to be pursued. Discernment gives power to your *no*. It allows you to listen to the Spirit, reflect on your priorities, and respond from a place of clarity.

Ask yourself:

- Does this align with my current season and calling?
- Will this move me forward or distract me?
- Am I saying *yes* out of fear or faith?
- What will this cost me in time, peace, or energy?

Don't just ask if you can do something. Ask if you should.

SUMMARY: CHAPTER TEN—KEY TAKEAWAYS

- Saying *no* is not selfish; it's strategic.

- Every *yes* has a cost. Be intentional with your commitments.

- Discernment is required to distinguish between distraction and direction.

- Boundaries protect your purpose and preserve your peace.

- You can say *no* with clarity, kindness, and confidence.

- Sometimes saying *no* to good is the only way to say *yes* to great.

- God leads through peace, not pressure.

- Your *no* creates space for God's best to flourish in your life.

"When you learn to say no to what's good, you make room for what's God."

CHAPTER 11

RESILIENCE: STAYING STRONG WHEN LIFE HITS HARD

"Fall seven times, stand up eight."
—JAPANESE PROVERB

LIFE DOESN'T ALWAYS GO ACCORDING TO PLAN

Life doesn't always go according to plan. The truth is, no matter how well you prepare, how clear your vision is, or how disciplined your actions are, life will eventually test your resolve. There will be seasons that blindside you; tragedies that break your heart; opportunities that fall through; battles you didn't see coming. Discipline alone isn't enough to carry you through these moments. You need something deeper. You need resilience.

Even the most focused, disciplined, and purpose-driven people experience setbacks, losses, and unexpected blows. The road to success isn't a straight line; it's filled with detours, delays, and disappointments. Every great story includes chapters of pain and pages of perseverance. That's why Focused Discipline is not just about momentum; it's about resilience. Momentum may start your journey; resilience is what finishes it.

WHAT RESILIENCE REALLY MEANS

Resilience is the capacity to bounce back: not in denial of what happened, but in defiance of defeat. It's the inner grit to keep going when everything in you wants to give up. It's the quiet courage to show up again, believe again, try again. Resilience doesn't mean you never feel pain; it means you choose to rise despite it. It's the decision to rise, again and again, no matter how many times life knocks you down. It's not powered by emotion; it's powered by conviction.

Without resilience, discipline won't last. The moment pressure comes, passion fizzles. The minute things get hard, habits crumble. With resilience, even the harshest seasons can become stepping stones to strength. The worst days can produce your greatest growth. Your darkest valley can lead to your highest victory. When you anchor your life in purpose and resolve, no storm can shake your foundation. Resilience is more than survival: it's strength forged in adversity. It's hope that refuses to quit. It's Focused Discipline at its finest: determined, durable, and deeply rooted.

Resilience is not the absence of hardship; it's the strength to endure it without losing your identity or purpose. It's not about pretending you're okay when you're not. Remaining anchored even when the storm rages defines resilience. This internal resolve allows you to stand tall, even when everything around you shakes. Resilience embodies strength under pressure, faith under fire, and courage under strain. Resilient people don't avoid adversity; they grow through it. They understand that resistance is not their enemy; it's the environment in which their strength is formed.

Instead of asking, "Why me?" they ask, "What now?" They are not defined by what happens to them, but by what they choose to do in response. True resilience is built on perspective. Choosing to see every trial as temporary rather than permanent is crucial. Recognizing that setbacks are often setups for what's next is essential. Realizing that delays are not denials but often divine recalibrations is key. When your perspective shifts from pain to purpose, everything changes. You don't get to choose all your circumstances; however, you do get to choose your response. That response shapes your future. It determines whether you retreat or rise, whether you stagnate or stretch.

PAIN IS PART OF THE PROCESS

Resilience is not a personality trait; it's a practiced mindset. Each day, you make the decision to keep showing up with integrity, faith, and focus, even when your feelings don't cooperate. That's the essence of Focused Discipline under pressure. Discipline doesn't make you immune to pain; it prepares you to handle it well. Every great journey includes hard days. Every champion has scars. Pain doesn't disqualify you from your purpose; in many cases, it deepens it.

Think about the gym. Strength builds through resistance. Growth comes from stretching and sometimes tearing muscle fibers so they can repair stronger. The same is true for your spirit. Every difficulty presents an opportunity to deepen your roots. Pain reveals what's unshakable. It exposes what's real. It strips away superficial motivations and forces you to reconnect with your deeper why. Don't waste your pain; let it purify your purpose.

STAYING GROUNDED WHEN LIFE SHAKES YOU

When life hits hard, your ability to stay grounded depends on your foundation. Just as a tree relies on deep roots to stand firm in a storm, so too must you anchor yourself in something deeper than emotion or external circumstances. That's why disciplines like prayer, journaling, reflection, and engaging with community matter. These aren't just spiritual habits; they're anchors that stabilize you in turbulent seasons.

Prayer connects you to God's strength when yours is failing. It's more than a religious ritual; it's a lifeline. Prayer realigns your spirit, reminds you of God's presence, and renews your inner strength. Like Jesus in Gethsemane, prayer is where you gather resolve before facing the battle.

JOURNALING

Journaling helps you process your emotions with honesty and clarity. When life feels chaotic, writing down your thoughts creates structure. It gives language to pain, clarity to confusion, and insight to experiences. Journaling is where pain becomes perspective.

REFLECTION

Reflection reminds you of past victories and God's faithfulness. It's the discipline of remembering. Like David recalling how God helped him defeat the lion and the bear before facing Goliath, reflection equips you with confidence that if God did it before, He can do it again.

COMMUNITY

Community surrounds you with encouragement when isolation tempts you to give up. Life was never meant to be lived alone. When trials strike, the support of trusted friends, mentors, or a faith community can speak life, lend strength, and remind you that you're not alone. Elijah found this in the wilderness when God sent an angel and later a companion in Elisha.

SPIRITUAL DISCIPLINES

Imagine a ship sailing through a storm. If it has no anchor, it will drift and may be destroyed. If the anchor is deep and secure, the ship might rock, but it won't be lost. That's what spiritual disciplines do for your soul; they anchor you when everything else is shaking. Storms will come. That's a guarantee. When your roots go deep, the storm won't uproot you. It may bend you. It may bruise you. It may feel like you're barely holding on. If you're grounded in truth, anchored in discipline, and surrounded by the right voices, it won't break you. You'll rise stronger, deeper, and more focused than before.

WHAT RESILIENT PEOPLE DO DIFFERENTLY

Resilient people are not superhuman. They feel pain, they experience loss, and they battle discouragement. They cry. They question. They wrestle with doubt and disappointment. Here's what sets them apart: they don't stay stuck. They learn to rise even when rising feels impossible.

1. They Give Themselves Permission to Feel

They don't numb or deny emotion; they process it in healthy ways. Ignoring pain doesn't make it disappear; it makes it grow silently. They cry when they need to cry. They talk when they need to talk. They grieve without shame and feel without apology. This emotional honesty becomes their path to healing.

2. They Refuse to Let Failure Define Them

A bad day doesn't make a bad life. A failed attempt doesn't make a failed person. When they fall short, they don't label themselves as broken; they see themselves as becoming. They separate their identity from their performance. Failure, to them, is feedback, not finality.

3. They Stay Committed to Growth

Even when progress is slow, they keep learning, reflecting, and improving. They treat life as a classroom and view adversity as an education. Whether it's reading, journaling, asking questions, or applying lessons from mistakes, resilient people are always in pursuit of becoming better, not just stronger.

4. They Anchor to Truth

They don't build on feelings or trends; they build on values and purpose. Their stability doesn't come from circumstances but from convictions. When emotions scream doubt, they return to the truth they know about God, about themselves, and about their calling.

5. They Speak Life Over Themselves

Their internal dialogue is one of faith, not fear; hope, not despair. They know that self-talk shapes self-perception, so they declare God's promises over their pain. They don't wait for others to affirm them; they remind themselves of who they are.

6. They Make Space for Restoration

Resilient people know they need to recharge. They take rest seriously. They step away to breathe, reflect, and recalibrate. They're not afraid to slow down when needed, knowing that true strength is sustained, not forced.

7. They Find Purpose in the Pain

They ask, "What can this teach me?" instead of "Why is this happening?" They see every challenge as part of a larger narrative. Their pain becomes fuel, not an obstacle. In time, that pain becomes part of their power.

RESILIENCE AND STRENGTH

Resilient people don't fake strength; they cultivate it. Day by day, choice by choice, they develop the muscle of perseverance. They don't wait for perfect conditions; they learn to thrive through imperfect ones. Their lives are not marked by how easy it's been, rather by how committed they've been to rise through every challenge.

BOUNCE-BACK MOMENTS: TURNING SETBACKS INTO SETUPS

Setbacks are inevitable. They don't have to be permanent. In fact, some of the most powerful stories of transformation begin in moments of disappointment. One of the greatest displays of resilience is the ability to turn a setback into a setup; a platform for greater clarity, character, and capacity. That shift doesn't happen by accident. It begins with a change in mindset.

- What can I learn from this?
- How can I grow through this?
- What does this challenge reveal about what I need to strengthen?

REDIRECTING YOUR FOCUS

These questions redirect your focus from the pain of the moment to the potential within it. Instead of spiraling into self-pity or blame, you begin to mine your experience for wisdom, maturity, and purpose. Every comeback starts with a decision; not to deny reality, rather to rise in the face of it.

EXAMPLES OF RESILIENCE

Consider Joseph in the Bible. Betrayed by his brothers, sold into slavery, falsely accused, and thrown into prison; his life was a series of brutal setbacks. Yet through every disappointment, he remained faithful. His character was forged in the furnace of adversity. When the time came, he didn't just survive; he led. His setback became the setup for the salvation of a nation.

Or think of an entrepreneur who launches a business that fails. At first, the loss is devastating. In reflection, they gain insight; on leadership, on communication, on systems. They learn what not to do. They mature emotionally. They discover their true strengths. When they launch again, it's with greater wisdom and resilience. Some of your greatest insights, innovations, and breakthroughs will come not from your victories, rather from your valleys. That's where resilience is forged; not in the comfort of success, but in the grit of getting back up.

SEEING SETBACKS AS REFINING POINTS

When you adopt this perspective, you stop seeing setbacks as roadblocks. You start seeing them as refining points. God often does His deepest work in your life not when everything is going right; rather, it is when everything feels like it's falling apart. Your valley may be the very thing God uses to launch you into your next level. Your pain may be preparing you for a platform. Your loss may become your message. If you allow Him, God will turn your setback into a setup—not just for a comeback, but for a transformation.

WHEN YOUR FAITH FEELS TESTED

There are seasons when you wonder, "Where is God in all of this?" Your prayers seem unanswered. Your plans fall apart. Your emotions feel raw. Your strength is depleted; even your spiritual disciplines feel dry. In these moments, faith and resilience don't feel like grand declarations; they feel like quiet whispers of endurance.

This is exactly where faith and resilience meet: in the tension between your expectation and your current experience. Hebrews 10:36 says, "You need to persevere so that when you have done the will of God, you will receive what He has promised." Notice, it doesn't say that God will spare you from hard seasons; it says perseverance is required in order to receive the promise. This reminds us that the journey of faith is not always filled with mountaintop moments. Sometimes, it's marked by long valleys and lonely nights. God is not absent in your adversity. He's present in your perseverance.

Sometimes the miracle isn't the removal of the problem; it's the endurance to walk through it. Like Shadrach, Meshach, and Abednego in the fiery furnace, God may not take you out of the fire; He will meet you in it. When He does, the flames lose their power to destroy you. Your resilience becomes your testimony—not because you avoided the fire, but because you overcame it with your faith intact.

Jesus Himself endured the cross, for He saw the joy on the other side (Hebrews 12:2). He didn't quit when it got hard. He didn't shrink back when it got painful. He pressed on through betrayal, through agony, through isolation; His motivation came from a higher calling. Your ability to press on is a reflection of His strength in you.

THE NATURE OF FAITH

Faith doesn't always look like bold declarations. Sometimes, it looks like waking up and choosing to believe again. It's praying again after silence. It's trusting again after disappointment. It's staying in position when everything in you wants to run. That's resilience born of faith.

In the testing of your faith, your spiritual roots grow deeper. Your dependence on God becomes real. Your trust is refined, not in what He can do for you, but in who He is to you. This is how resilient faith is formed: in the crucible of testing, where easy answers fade and deep trust emerges.

EMOTIONAL RESILIENCE: GUARDING YOUR INNER LIFE

Resilience is not just physical; it's emotional. Emotional fatigue is one of the biggest enemies of consistent discipline. When your internal world is overloaded, even the best plans crumble. Building and guarding emotional resilience is vital to long-term success.

Recognize emotional overload. Don't ignore the signs of burnout, bitterness, or buried frustration. Like the warning lights on a car dashboard, these emotions signal the need for attention. If left unaddressed, they will short-circuit your motivation and clarity. Learn to check in with yourself regularly. Ask, "What am I feeling, and why?"

DEVELOP HEALTHY OUTLETS

You can't pour out endlessly without replenishing. Talk to mentors who can provide perspective. Take walks to clear your mind. Engage in creative rest—whether through music, art, journaling, or simply doing something that recharges your soul. Don't just power through; process through. Recovery isn't a reward for work; it's part of the work.

PRACTICE SELF-COMPASSION

Speak to yourself with the same grace you'd extend to a friend. That inner critic that says you're failing? Replace it with truth. Progress doesn't demand perfection; it demands persistence. Stay optimistic; the future holds great promise. You can be hurting and still moving forward. Treat yourself with the healing and gentleness God offers you.

THE ROLE OF HABITS IN BUILDING RESILIENCE

Imagine a high-performing athlete. Behind every record-breaking performance is a regimen of recovery: ice baths, sleep, stretching, mental coaching. Emotional resilience works the same way. Admitting you're tired is not a sign of weakness; it demonstrates wisdom in taking care of your soul for the long haul. Your emotional life matters. Protect it. Nourish it. Build rituals around replenishment. When it wavers, don't isolate; recalibrate. Sometimes your greatest breakthrough comes not from pushing harder; it arises from pulling back to rest, reflect, and renew.

When crisis hits, you don't rise to the level of your feelings; you fall to the level of your systems. In moments of chaos, it's not your emotions that keep you steady; it's your routines. That's why daily habits matter. They serve as scaffolding, supporting you when everything else feels shaky. Think of habits as anchors during storms. When the winds of adversity blow, your habits hold you steady. When you're tired, disoriented, or emotionally drained, you default to what you've consistently practiced. That default—if built with intention—can save your progress, your peace, and even your purpose.

MORNING ROUTINES GROUND YOUR DAY

Starting with prayer, gratitude, or a moment of silence aligns your heart and mind before the demands of the world hit. This practice signals that you are living from the inside out, not the outside in.

EXERCISE RELEASES TENSION

Physical movement is more than fitness; it's therapy. It clears mental fog, boosts emotional well-being, and reminds your body that it is still alive, strong, and capable of showing up.

READING AND REFLECTION SHARPEN YOUR MIND

Consuming wisdom daily, whether through Scripture, books, or personal insights, keeps your spirit anchored and your thinking elevated. Reflection turns experiences into insight, and insight into growth.

SCHEDULED REST RESTORES YOUR STRENGTH

Rest isn't a luxury; it's a strategy. Even machines need maintenance. Your soul requires space to breathe. Protect your Sabbath moments. Prioritize sleep. Practice rhythms of rest.

These habits don't need to be glamorous to be effective. Even small daily actions compound into massive inner strength over time. Like bricks in a wall, each habit reinforces the structure of your resilience. Consider a house built with reinforced beams. It may face wind, rain, or even tremors; however, due to its internal frame, it stands. Your habits are those internal beams. They are not optional; they are foundational. When you feel weak, return to your habits. When you're overwhelmed, lean on your rhythms. When motivation fades, let your systems carry you. Your daily disciplines become a survival kit in seasons of uncertainty. Habits are the guardrails that keep you moving forward even when the road feels steep. In time, what once required effort becomes your default. That's when resilience stops being reactive and becomes a lifestyle of strength.

LET GOD REDEEM YOUR BROKEN PLACES

One of the most powerful truths about resilience is this: God doesn't waste your pain. He redeems it. He restores what was lost. He uses your scars as stories, your losses as lessons, and your setbacks as stages for His glory. Romans 8:28 reminds us, "All things work together for good to those who love God, to those who are called according to His purpose." That includes the hard things, the things you didn't choose, and the moments that broke your heart. You are not defined by what you've been through. You are refined by it.

SUMMARY: CHAPTER ELEVEN—KEY TAKEAWAYS

- Resilience is not the absence of pain; it's the ability to rise through it.

- Focused discipline requires strength for the long haul, especially in hard seasons.

- Pain is not a disqualifier; it's often a deepener of purpose.

- Resilient people feel deeply, yet they stay rooted in truth and growth.

- Emotional resilience must be protected through healthy outlets and rest.

- Habits are the invisible structures that carry you when motivation is low.

- God redeems every broken piece when you give it to Him.

"Resilience is not about bouncing back to who you were; it's about rising into who you're becoming."

CHAPTER 12

ATTITUDE IS EVERYTHING

"Your attitude, not your aptitude, will determine your altitude."

—ZIG ZIGLAR

There's a reason attitude is often called the difference-maker. It's not just a catchy phrase; it's a life principle. Your attitude determines how you interpret life, how you respond to pressure, and how you recover from failure. In business, leadership, marriage, and faith, your attitude either becomes a bridge to breakthrough or a wall that blocks it. You can have all the right credentials. You can have incredible vision. Opportunities may knock at your door. If your attitude is sour, inconsistent, defensive, or easily shaken, you'll sabotage your own progress. Why? People may be drawn to your talent; they stay because of your attitude.

ILLUSTRATING THE DIFFERENCE

Let me illustrate this. Years ago, I mentored two young sales professionals. Both were brilliant. Both had charisma. One consistently rose while the other floundered. The difference wasn't their skill; it was their attitude. One embraced every challenge as an opportunity to grow. The other complained, blamed others, and doubted their own value. The one with the better attitude wasn't always the top seller, but he was always the one that clients remembered. He became trustworthy, resilient, and consistent due to how he saw adversity. That's the power of attitude.

FORMING YOUR ATTITUDE

Attitude is not fixed. It's formed. No one is born with a positive or negative attitude. It's shaped over time by what you think about, what you dwell on, and what you choose to believe about yourself, others, and your situation. You might not choose what happens to you; you do choose the story you tell yourself about it. That internal story is what forms your emotional posture.

Your attitude stems from a simple yet powerful chain: Thoughts → Feelings → Actions → Outcomes.

It begins in your thoughts. What you think about consistently shapes how you feel. Your feelings influence your actions. Your actions create results. If you want different outcomes, don't start by forcing new behaviors. Start by rewiring the thoughts that drive them. Begin with belief. Your internal posture determines your external performance. That's why two people can face the same situation and come out with two very different results. One sees the obstacle and shuts down. The other sees the same obstacle and rises up. The external remains the same; the difference lies within. It's attitude.

EMOTIONAL AGILITY

When your attitude is strong, you become emotionally agile. You're not easily offended. You don't shrink in rejection. You stay focused when others spiral. You move with grounded faith rather than unstable emotion. Over time, that mental and emotional consistency becomes your superpower. Attitude is the engine behind Focused Discipline. If your mindset is poor, your discipline will crumble. A rich mindset, full of hope, purpose, and resilience, makes your discipline sustainable.

WHAT IS ATTITUDE, REALLY?

Attitude is the lens through which you see the world. It's the internal compass that directs your response to challenges, rejection, opportunities, and people. Where some see failure, others see a lesson. Where some feel overwhelmed, others see potential. The difference is not their intelligence or upbringing; it's their attitude. A positive, faith-filled attitude isn't about pretending problems don't exist. It's not about suppressing feelings or denying facts. It's about choosing a perspective rooted in truth, hope, and expectation. It's choosing to believe that today's hardship can produce tomorrow's wisdom. That pain has purpose. That every day holds potential.

On the other hand, a negative attitude filters everything through a lens of defeat, fear, or cynicism. It exaggerates problems and minimizes possibilities. It's quick to blame and slow to believe. A negative attitude doesn't just affect your emotions; it erodes your decision-making, dims your vision, and pushes away opportunity.

A LESSON FROM THE ISRAELITES

Take the Israelites as an example. In Numbers 13, twelve spies were sent to scout the Promised Land. Ten came back with fear-filled, negative reports. "We seemed like grasshoppers in our own eyes; we looked the same to them" (Numbers 13:33). Only two, Joshua and Caleb, returned with faith. Same land. Same giants. Different attitudes. As a result, only two entered the promise. That's how powerful attitude is. It determines whether you possess the promise or retreat in fear.

THE SALES PERSPECTIVE

When I began in sales, I quickly learned this: people don't just buy your product, they buy your attitude. If you believe in what you offer, that belief shows up. Carrying discouragement or entitlement reveals itself as well. Your attitude leaks. It informs every email you write, every room you enter, every call you make.

Scripture affirms this principle repeatedly: Romans 12:2 urges us to "be transformed by the renewing of your mind." That renewal shapes our attitude.

THE MIND OF CHRIST

Philippians 2:5 says, "Let this mind be in you which was also in Christ Jesus." His mindset embodied humility, obedience, and unwavering focus.

SPIRITUAL MATURITY

1 Thessalonians 5:16–18 reminds us: "Rejoice always, pray continually, give thanks in all circumstances." That's not emotional denial; it's spiritual maturity.

ATTITUDE: A SPIRITUAL DISCIPLINE

Attitude, then, is deeply spiritual. It's not a personality trait but a discipline. A heart trained to see possibilities. A mind conditioned to expect the best, prepare for the test, and endure through the rest. It's choosing joy over bitterness, courage over fear, and faith over facts. This kind of attitude doesn't happen by accident; it's cultivated. It changes everything.

GRATITUDE: THE DAILY RESET

If attitude is a muscle, then gratitude is your daily workout. Gratitude serves as the reset button for your perspective. It pulls you back from the edge of frustration and realigns you with what matters most. Ideal conditions are not required; intentional vision is necessary. Gratitude is not about pretending everything is perfect. It's about finding the gold in the middle of the grind. It's about noticing the small wins, the unseen blessings, and the daily miracles we often overlook due to fixation on what's next.

Every morning, I start with gratitude. Before checking emails, before strategy calls, and before meetings, I list what I'm thankful for. Sometimes it's big: my health, wife, daughter, family, business, church family, freedom, sunrise, and my calling. Sometimes it's small: a good night's sleep, a productive day yesterday, or a kind word from someone unexpected. Every time, it lifts my spirit and sets the tone.

Gratitude matters so much. It stops negativity in its tracks. It interrupts the spiral of worry and silences the voice of complaint. It reminds you of what's true, even when you feel overwhelmed. Gratitude doesn't ignore difficulty; it puts difficulty in perspective. Think of it like adjusting the lens on a camera. Gratitude doesn't change what's in the frame; it changes the clarity with which you see it. It zooms in on goodness, on faithfulness, on what's already working.

In 1 Thessalonians 5:18, Paul instructs us to "give thanks in all circumstances." Not for all things, but in all things. Thanksgiving creates alignment. It opens your heart to God's presence, even in hardship. It unlocks joy and keeps you rooted. I've seen teams transform simply by introducing a culture of gratitude. Morale lifted, conflict lessened, and energy surged. Gratitude blesses everyone it touches, not just the person who practices it.

Gratitude is also a spiritual weapon. It defeats entitlement, dismantles fear, and builds faith. Psalm 100:4 tells us to "enter His gates with thanksgiving and His courts with praise." In other words, gratitude is how we gain access to God's presence. It's not just nice; it's necessary. So make this a non-negotiable in your life. Before your day accelerates, pause and list five things you're grateful for. Do it consistently, when you feel like it, and especially when you don't. Watch how your focus sharpens. Watch how your heart lifts. Watch how your attitude realigns. Gratitude is not just a feeling; it's a discipline. It's one of the most powerful disciplines you can build.

FOCUSED DISCIPLINE

WHEN REJECTION FEELS PERSONAL

Let's talk about one of the hardest realities in business: rejection. You pour your energy into a pitch. You prepare with excellence. You believe in the value you bring. Then, the answer is *no*. Or worse, silence. If you're not careful, that rejection doesn't just bounce off your work; it burrows into your identity. I've lived this. I've heard it more times than I can count.

Here's what I learned: rejection is not always about you. Sometimes it's about timing. It may involve budgets or the client's mindset or season. Rejection in business is rarely a rejection of your worth; it's simply data. Even if the rejection is personal, it's still not permanent. To maintain a strong attitude in a rejection-heavy environment, you must develop resilience.

Here are some strategies that helped me:

- **Detach identity from outcome.** You are not your sales numbers. You are not your last email open rate. You are not your closing ratio. You are a person of value with or without a sale.

- **Ask What You Can Learn.** Every rejection is a teacher. Was the pitch too early? Was the client not the right fit? Did I miss a need? Learn and adjust.

- **Have a "Who's Next" Mindset. Don't dwell on the no.** Keep moving. Keep prospecting. Someone out there needs exactly what you offer. A closed door shouldn't prevent you from knocking on the next.

THE "THIS IS THE DAY" PRACTICE

Psalm 118:24 says, "This is the day the Lord has made. We will rejoice and be glad in it." It is a verse I practice. It's my daily declaration. It's my perspective reset. Every day you wake up, you have a choice. You can dread the day, or you can declare it. You can let circumstances dictate your emotions, or you can let gratitude and vision guide them. This verse does not suggest that every day will be easy; rather, it emphasizes that every day is sacred and filled with divine potential.

Here's how I apply this practically:

1. **Wake up and speak the verse aloud.** Even when I don't feel like it. Especially when I don't feel like it. Saying it aloud affirms your authority over the day. It sets a spiritual tone. It declares your intention to see the day through a lens of faith and possibility, not fear or fatigue. Your voice carries power. When you declare the Word of God, it doesn't just inform your mind; it transforms your mindset.

2. **Choose one reason to rejoice.** Even in stressful seasons, there's always something. Life. Family. Purpose. A breakthrough you're believing for. A lesson learned. Rejoicing doesn't mean ignoring pain; it means placing gratitude beside it. Choosing joy shifts your emotional chemistry and prepares your spirit to lead, not lag.

3. **Refuse to let yesterday define today.** Every day is a fresh page. Start it with hope. Don't drag yesterday's disappointment into today's momentum. God's mercies are new every morning (Lamentations 3:23). So is your opportunity to think differently, act boldly, and expect divine results. The failures of the past do not get to narrate the story of today unless you let them.

THE POWER OF MINDSET

This one practice has saved me countless times from spiraling into negativity. It doesn't erase pressure; it gives me perspective. It reminds me that I'm not alone, that each day is a gift, and that forward motion, no matter how small, is still motion.

WHY MINDSET IS A BUSINESS ASSET

Your mindset is one of your greatest assets in business. It drives your tone, your energy, your adaptability, and your creative problem-solving. When your mindset is strong, your strategy becomes sharper. A weak mindset causes even the best strategy to collapse under pressure. Focused discipline encompasses both external consistency and internal maturity. Your attitude doesn't just affect your productivity; it determines your longevity. People with poor attitudes burn out. Those with trained attitudes rise, recover, and keep building. Think about it this way: skills are teachable. Knowledge is transferable. You don't stumble into a strong attitude. You grow it. You train it. You keep it close, like a treasure.

PROTECTING YOUR ATTITUDE DAILY

You don't need a perfect day to have a powerful attitude. You need consistent inputs. Here are practical ways to protect your attitude:

- Limit toxic inputs. What you consume affects how you feel. Turn down the noise: social media, bad news, negative conversations. Protect your mental and emotional space.

- Practice reflection. Take time to ask: Where did my attitude shift today? What lifted me? What drained me? Awareness leads to adjustment.

- Surround yourself with positive voices. Who shapes your mindset? Be around people who speak life, challenge growth, and model resilience.

FOCUSED DISCIPLINE

TRAINING YOUR THOUGHTS

The apostle Paul said in Philippians 4:8 to think on things that are true, noble, right, pure, lovely, admirable, excellent, and praiseworthy. This serves as a training manual for everyday attitude. If your thoughts create your feelings and your feelings drive your actions, then your thinking is the root. Guard it. Feed it with truth. Align it with heaven.

During one of the most challenging seasons in my business, my attitude carried me through. I told myself daily: "This is building me. This is preparing me. This is not the end of the story." I believed it long enough for the season to shift. At the core of Focused Discipline lies the conviction that external results stem from internal resolve. Attitude is not just a soft skill; it's a survival skill.

In sales, ministry, entrepreneurship, and leadership, attitude fuels your progress when motivation fades. You don't control everything that happens; however, you control how you show up. Choose to arrive with courage, clarity, joy, vision, and honor. That choice, made daily, will shape your future more than any tactic ever could.

SUMMARY: CHAPTER TWELVE—ATTITUDE IS EVERYTHING

- Your attitude determines how far you go more than your talent or opportunity.

- Gratitude serves as the most powerful reset for perspective and energy.

- Rejection in business is inevitable; it's not personal; it's data.

- "This is the day the Lord has made" represents a mindset, not just a memory verse.

- Protect your inputs, train your thoughts, and choose perspective daily.

- Your attitude leaks; lead with one that inspires.

- Focused Discipline flows from a heart trained to rejoice, even when it's hard.

"You may not control the storm, but you can control your spirit. That control is what makes you unstoppable."

CHAPTER 13

MARRIAGE AND MISSION; PARTNERING FOR PURPOSE

"If you want to go fast, go alone; if you want to go far, go together."
—AFRICAN PROVERB

Behind every focused individual who finishes strong, there is often a team. In my case, the most powerful partner in purpose I've had is my wife. Marrying the right person can transform your entire trajectory. It is one of the most consequential decisions you will ever make. Your spouse has the power to either reinforce your calling or drain your energy. When the person beside you believes in you, covers you in prayer, calls out the best in you, and shares in your vision, you gain more than emotional support; you gain a strategic advantage. You gain a partner in purpose.

Marriage isn't a distraction from the mission. It can be the fuel that sustains it. A strong marriage adds weight to your words, structure to your vision, and peace to your environment. It becomes the invisible strength behind visible success. When done with alignment, humility, and shared values, marriage offers an irreplaceable sense of grounding.

FOCUSED DISCIPLINE AT HOME

Focused Discipline doesn't just happen in boardrooms or on sales calls. It starts in the home. When Jennifer and I began this journey together, we weren't entering into just a romantic relationship; we were entering a covenant rooted in calling. We were saying *yes* to a shared destiny, to a future we would build with intentionality.

I quickly learned that the same principles that kept me grounded in business—clarity, consistency, and communication—were just as necessary in marriage. I also discovered that the fruits of those principles were even more beautiful when nurtured in the soil of love, respect, and faith.

HARRIS D. McFARLARE

HOW MY WIFE BECAME MY GREATEST SUPPORT

From the earliest days, Jennifer saw more in me than I saw in myself. She believed in the vision before the results came in. She didn't just love me; she lent me strength when I felt weak. When I wrestled with uncertainty, she reminded me who I was and why we started. That kind of support is priceless. She prayed when I didn't have words. She organized when I felt overwhelmed. She stood in faith when I was tempted to give up.

Most importantly, she never let my identity be defined by performance. In a world where so many leaders are only celebrated when producing, Jennifer reminded me that my worth wasn't in what I did; it was in who I was. Jennifer didn't try to compete with my mission; she co-labored with it. Her role as a wife was never a background character; it was central to the stability that allowed me to thrive.

She became the sounding board for big ideas, the voice of calm in high-stress seasons, and the anchor that held me steady when the waves of leadership threatened to knock me off course. If you are an entrepreneur or leader, do not underestimate the value of a spouse who supports your mission. If you are married, invest time in building that unity. Share your vision. Invite your spouse into the story—not just to observe it; involve them in shaping it with you.

Listen to their wisdom. Pray with them regularly. Create rhythms of rest and communication that allow your relationship to be the sanctuary fueling your calling. If you are not yet married, be prayerful and intentional about whom you choose. Marrying the right person is not just about chemistry; it is about calling and discernment. A partner who aligns with your purpose will multiply your focus, not distract from it. They will sharpen your thinking, strengthen your faith, and give you a reason to keep showing up even when it's hard. Focused Discipline is sustained when you are surrounded by the right voices; no voice matters more than the one you come home to.

HER ROLE IN ADMINISTRATION AND THE HOME FRONT

We often celebrate public success without realizing the quiet systems that support it. Jennifer took charge of the areas that required steady leadership: finances, scheduling, communication, and day-to-day logistics that allowed me to focus. At home, she created an atmosphere of love, peace, and faith for me and Nicole. Her ability to lead on the home front freed me up for bigger responsibilities. More than that, she showed me that strength doesn't have to be loud to be powerful.

We developed rhythms. We prayed together, planned weekly, and took short getaways to realign. These practices allowed us to stay unified and focused.

IMPACT OF PARTNERSHIP ON STAYING FOCUSED

Focused discipline is hard to sustain in isolation. Even the most driven individuals face moments of doubt, discouragement, and fatigue. Some days, motivation may dry up, outcomes may not match effort, and the dream once carried so passionately can feel more like a burden than a blessing. In those moments, having a partner who understands the vision and carries it with you becomes invaluable.

Jennifer has been that partner for me. She reminds me of the purpose when I get lost in the pressure. She also equips me by offering insight, asking the right questions, and challenging me when needed. When your spouse can see both your blind spots and your brilliance, and speaks to both with grace, you grow in ways you never could on your own.

Jennifer and I learned early on that the mission wasn't "his" or "hers." It was ours. We stewarded it together. When a big decision arose, we talked it out. We didn't rush to fix things; we paused to pray. We brought our different perspectives to the table and treated each other as equals in purpose, even when our responsibilities differed. When obstacles hit, we strategized together. We didn't just react; we responded with faith and wisdom.

That unity didn't just protect our marriage; it multiplied our impact. There were times I was on the verge of burnout; her insight brought balance. She didn't try to rescue me; she created space for me to reset. Some seasons required her to carry more of the load—times when my plate was full with launching projects or navigating tough transitions. Other seasons called for me to support her more closely. Through it all, we refused to let pressure divide us. Instead, we chose to let the pressure deepen our bond, refine our communication, and remind us why we started.

Every entrepreneur needs someone who not only claps when they win but also stands when they wobble. That's the power of purposeful partnership. It doesn't just keep you focused; it helps you remember who you are and why your work matters.

EXAMPLES OF TEAMWORK AND RESILIENCE

There were seasons when life was moving fast. The weight of responsibility felt heavier than usual. In one of those moments, I was preparing for a major church event while navigating a tight deadline for a business proposal. During that time, I found myself emotionally and physically stretched. Jennifer helped and led. She arranged our schedule to allow me time to focus. She fielded calls, managed meals, and still ensured we had moments of encouragement in between. Her calm presence under pressure reminded me that I wasn't doing this alone.

That season could have been chaotic. Instead, it revealed the strength of our partnership. We didn't have all the answers; we had each other. That unity created focus. Ecclesiastes 4:9–10 says, "Two are better than one… If either of them falls down, one can help the other up." Those words became a foundation we stood on, not just an idea we quoted.

Partnership is not about being identical; it's about being intentional. It involves celebrating your differences and using them as strength. Jennifer didn't need to be in the spotlight to be essential. Her faith, steadiness, and sacrificial love carried us through. If you're married or planning to be, let me say this: Don't chase your dream at the expense of your spouse. Bring them into the dream. Honor their voice. Value their input. Celebrate their contribution; success is sweetest when shared.

FAITH AND FOCUS IN THE MARRIAGE JOURNEY

One thing I have discovered is that shared faith strengthens shared focus. When Jennifer and I make decisions together in prayer, the peace that follows is different. Studying the Word together aligns our thinking. Bringing our frustrations before God instead of fighting each other preserves unity.

Marriage is a covenant, not a contract. Covenant thrives in clarity, commitment, and compassion. You are not always going to agree. You are not always going to be in the same emotional space; Focused Discipline means showing up even when it's inconvenient. It means serving even when you're tired. It means protecting the mission by protecting each other. There's a reason Scripture says, "A cord of three strands is not easily broken." That third strand is God. He strengthens the bond. He fills the gaps. He makes the ordinary partnership sacred.

SUMMARY: CHAPTER THIRTEEN—MARRIAGE AND MISSION

- A strong marriage will fuel your mission, not hinder it.

- Partnership requires intentional communication, shared values, spiritual alignment, and commitment.

- The quiet systems at home often determine public success in business or ministry.

- Don't underestimate the power of a praying spouse.

- Shared faith leads to shared focus; shared focus multiplies impact.

- Protect your marriage; your mission will go further.

"Two are better than one… if either falls, the other can help them up." (Ecclesiastes 4:9–10)

Partnership multiplies potential. Reflect on how your relationships support your purpose. Reach out to someone who shares your values and discuss ways to encourage each other's discipline.

CHAPTER 14

OBJECTION DOESN'T MEAN REJECTION

"Failure is delay, not defeat."
—UNKNOWN

One of the biggest hurdles in sales, entrepreneurship, and leadership is learning how to deal with rejection. It touches everyone—from seasoned CEOs to first-time sales reps. Here's the truth: rejection isn't personal—it's often situational. Even more important, objection doesn't mean rejection.

UNDERSTANDING OBJECTION

Let's define objection clearly. An objection is a statement, concern, or resistance raised by a person in response to a product, proposal, or idea. It's not always a definitive *no*. Rather, it's often a reflection of doubt, lack of clarity, timing, or the need for more information. In other words, objections are signals. They point to areas where more communication, connection, or clarity is needed. Objection can also be seen as a form of engagement. The person hasn't disengaged—they're giving you feedback. They're opening a door to dialogue. That's powerful.

Think of it this way: rejection is often final; objection is fluid. It can be turned into opportunity with the right posture. That posture is grounded in Focused Discipline. In fact, some of the best business relationships I've developed started with a firm *no*. At first, it might sting. You prepare your pitch, make the call, present your value, and still hear the words: "Not interested." That moment can feel deflating.

REJECTION AS A PART OF THE PROCESS

What I've learned—rejection is not the end of the story. It's part of the process. Often, it's a necessary step toward refinement and redirection. Rejection refines your message. It sharpens your delivery. It tests your resilience. It forces you to revisit your value and recalibrate your approach. If you allow it, it also deepens your character. Anyone can keep moving when applause follows them. It takes a different kind of person to move forward when doors close.

This is the soil where Focused Discipline grows. You learn to separate what you do from who you are. You learn to interpret feedback without internalizing failure. You begin to see that every *no* may just be a *not yet*. More importantly, you learn to trust the process—process builds people even when the result seems delayed.

THE POWER OF PERSPECTIVE

When you shift your mindset from taking objections personally to seeing them as feedback, everything changes. Objection becomes an open door—not a slammed one. It becomes an invitation to engage deeper, not a dismissal of your worth or ideas. Your perspective determines whether you walk away discouraged or lean in with curiosity.

Objection is an opportunity. It's a doorway to understanding your prospect better, refining your message, or even discovering what really matters to the person you're serving. I've learned that most people don't object to shut you down—they object because they don't yet feel understood. That shift alone can change everything.

Successful people don't collapse under *no*. They lean in. They ask better questions. They listen deeper. They learn faster. That's what Focused Discipline teaches you—to move forward with clarity even when the answer you expected isn't the one you receive.

BIBLICAL EXAMPLE OF HANDLING OBJECTION

Let's look at a biblical example: when Jesus spoke with the rich young ruler (Mark 10:17–22), the man asked what he needed to do to inherit eternal life. Jesus gave him the answer—sell everything and follow Him. The man walked away sorrowful. That was an objection. Jesus didn't chase him. He didn't panic. He honored the man's free will and stayed rooted in truth. That story reminds us: even perfect presentation and divine truth can still receive a *no*. That doesn't make the message invalid—it simply means the soil wasn't ready.

In business, leadership, or ministry, objection often signals that a person is processing. Give them space. Don't rush to fix. Instead, engage with compassion. Shift from performance mode to presence mode. Be available, not pushy. Be curious, not controlling. A good friend of mine once said, "Objection is just another word for 'I'm still thinking.'" That insight changed how I approached every sales conversation, every coaching relationship, and even how I offered help in ministry. When someone says, "I'm not sure," I don't interpret it as failure. I interpret it as formation.

EMBRACING REJECTION FOR GROWTH

This is where perspective becomes power. When you believe there is value even in rejection, you stop avoiding hard conversations. You start seeing every objection as a training ground for greater clarity and deeper empathy. Eventually, that mindset becomes a competitive edge—while others shrink back, you grow forward.

RESPONDING TO REJECTION

I've learned that how you respond to rejection reveals more about your maturity than your skillset. When someone declines your offer, what do you do? Do you give up? Do you assume the worst? Or do you reframe the moment? In sales, an objection might mean they don't yet see the value. In leadership, it might mean the timing is off. In ministry, it might mean God is still preparing their heart. None of these mean you're finished.

Here are a few healthy ways to respond when you hear no:

1. **Pause Before Reacting:** Don't rush to defend or justify. Breathe, reflect, and listen.

2. **Ask a Clarifying Question:** Sometimes a gentle, "Can you share more about what's holding you back?" opens up dialogue.

3. **Affirm Their Perspective**: Respect builds trust. Say, "I understand; it's important that this is the right fit for you."

4. **Reiterate Your Value**: Don't be afraid to confidently restate what you bring to the table without sounding pushy.

5. **Follow Up with Grace**: Leave the door open for future engagement. A kind message a few weeks later can reignite interest.

Jennifer often reminds me, "The 'no' you hear today is not a closed door—it's a call to recalibrate." That recalibration might be what leads to a deeper breakthrough later.

THE ART OF UNPACKING PROBLEMS

Most objections are not outright rejections—they're veiled problems. They are signals pointing to underlying fears, misunderstandings, or unmet needs. When someone says, "It's too expensive," they might really be saying, "I don't yet understand the value." When someone says, "I'm not ready," they might mean, "I'm afraid to take the leap." Objections are often less about you and more about what's unresolved in the mind or heart of the other person.

To truly serve others, you have to become a problem-solver, not just a product-pusher. Your role is not to push harder. It's to unpack the problem and explore the real issue behind the resistance. This requires empathy, patience, and discernment. It's about asking the right questions and listening without interrupting. When you do that, you gain insight that no script or pitch could ever provide.

Ask questions like:

- "What would need to be true for this to be a yes?"
- "What's your biggest hesitation?"
- "Is timing the issue or is it trust?"
- "What would make you feel more confident moving forward?"
- "What would a successful outcome look like for you?"

SHIFTING THE TONE OF CONVERSATION

These kinds of questions shift the tone of the conversation. You're no longer a seller; you're a solution partner. You're not trying to win them over; you're trying to help them win. One time, a client kept dodging my follow-ups. I finally asked, "Would it help if we scaled the package to better fit your timeline?" That single question opened up a 20-minute conversation about fears, budget, and pressure they felt from past experiences. By the end, we had a custom plan. That trust carried into future business.

THE EXAMPLE OF JESUS

Jesus was a master of unpacking problems. In John 4, when He met the Samaritan woman at the well, He didn't begin by correcting her or pushing a theological agenda. He started with a conversation. He listened and asked questions. He exposed her deeper need, her thirst for acceptance, identity, and truth. What began as an objection ("Why are you talking to me?") became a divine appointment. In business and ministry, the art of unpacking problems is the art of caring well. It's not about having all the answers; it's about asking the right questions until clarity emerges. Clarity often leads to connection. That connection is where trust is born and where transformation begins.

DON'T TAKE IT PERSONALLY

This is one of the hardest yet most important disciplines to develop. Separate your identity from the outcome. You are not your pitch. You are not your product. You are not your proposal. When you can detach from the emotional sting of a no, you stay empowered, present, and available for the next opportunity. Remember what Jesus told His disciples in Luke 10:16: "Whoever rejects you rejects me." In other words, rejection isn't about you; it's about the assignment. When you're walking in purpose, your job is to obey, not to force the result.

MINDSET: "WHO'S NEXT?"

I adopted this mindset early in my sales career. Instead of stewing over a lost deal, I'd simply say, "Who's next?" Not out of indifference, but out of confidence. I knew that someone out there needed what I carried. My job was to find them and stay ready. "Who's next?" reminds you that your supply is still needed. It gets your eyes off the closed door and onto the open field. It builds resilience. It activates momentum. When you choose movement over moping, you regain control of your energy. You realize that rejection is not a verdict—it's just feedback.

More than that, this mindset protects your joy. Instead of taking rejection as a personal loss, you reframe it as preparation for what's coming. I remember once following up with a prospect five times over eight months. Each time, they said *no*. On the sixth follow-up, something shifted. They were finally ready. That one *yes* became a relationship that lasted years and produced multiple referrals. What if I had quit after the third *no*?

What if I had taken it personally? Sometimes, the *yes* you're waiting for is just on the other side of one more faithful follow-up.

OBJECTION IS A TEST OF BELIEF

Every objection tests your belief—belief in your product, belief in your value, and most importantly, belief in yourself. If you don't believe in what you're offering, you'll shrink back at the first sign of resistance. When you are grounded in conviction, rejection doesn't rattle you. That's why Focused Discipline begins inside. Before you ever pitch to a client, you need to pitch to yourself. Remind yourself why what you offer matters. Rehearse the transformation your service or product provides. Strengthen your belief so it can carry you through the moments your results don't reflect your potential yet. Romans 5:3–4 says, "We glory in our sufferings, because we know that suffering produces perseverance; perseverance, character; and character, hope." Objection may not feel like suffering, but it does require perseverance. Every time you persevere, your character deepens and your hope expands.

CELEBRATE THE NO

This may sound strange, but I've learned to celebrate the *no*. Every *no* brings you closer to your next *yes*. Each *no* makes you better—sharper, more self-aware, more emotionally resilient. Instead of dreading rejection, expect it. Train for it. Respond with clarity and calm. There are lessons hidden in every objection:

What could I communicate more clearly next time?

Was I listening or just selling?

Did I rush the relationship?

When you mine the gold from every no, you elevate your next interaction. Your follow-up becomes more thoughtful. Your empathy grows. Confidence matures. I've often told my team, "Your goal is not just to close deals. It's to build relationships that lead to the right outcomes over time." This means not forcing results and trusting the process.

SUMMARY: KEY TAKEAWAYS

- Objection is not rejection. It's often a doorway to better understanding.

- Rejection is situational, not personal.

- How you respond to a no reveals your maturity and mindset.

- Unpack the real problem behind every objection through thoughtful questions.

- Don't tie your identity to your outcome.

- Reframe rejection as redirection and training.

- Adopt a "Who's next?" mindset to stay present and energized.

- Strengthen your belief before you step into the pitch.

- Celebrate the no—it's part of the process.

- Follow up with faith, focus, and humility.

A *no* today doesn't cancel your calling. It just redirects your path. Stay grounded. Stay disciplined. Stay available for the doors that are meant for you.

CHAPTER 15

ROOTED IN GOD – PRAYER, PROMISES, AND POWER

"Don't worry about anything; pray and ask God for everything you need, always giving thanks for what you have."
—PHILIPPIANS 4:6

Every great vision must be rooted in something deeper than hustle. Drive, ambition, and strategy may help you start; they are not enough to sustain you. Without a strong spiritual foundation, you'll eventually burn out, lose focus, or drift away from your original purpose. Purpose without power becomes pressure. Driving without direction leads to burnout. That's why Focused Discipline is not just a strategy; it's a spiritual posture.

At the center of that posture is your relationship with God. You can't fight spiritual battles with natural tools. You can't discern supernatural timing through human logic alone. Spiritual alignment is not optional; it's essential. The deeper your roots in God, the stronger your resilience, clarity, and capacity to stay the course. In a fast-moving world, prayer becomes your anchor. The promises of God become your blueprint. The power of the Holy Spirit becomes your fuel.

When your identity is rooted in who God says you are, your decisions become less reactive and more responsive to His leading. You weren't meant to live life solely on human strength. You were designed to partner with divine power. As Zechariah 4:6 reminds us, "Not by might, nor by power, but by my Spirit, says the Lord of hosts." True impact comes from partnership with God; not performance for people. Think of your life like a tree. Your fruitfulness is determined by your root system. If your roots are shallow, adversity will uproot you. If your roots run deep in God, you can weather any season and still produce fruit at the right time.

GOD IS OUR CHAIRMAN AND CEO

In our business and ministry, we've often said this: "God is our Chairman and CEO." That's not a slogan; it's a truth we live by. It means we don't operate based on pressure or public opinion. We operate under divine leadership. Every major decision is preceded by prayer. Every strategic direction is filtered through Scripture. Every challenge is brought before the throne of grace before it's presented in the boardroom.

There were seasons when we were running on faith and fumes. Resources were thin. We faced closed doors and uncertain next steps. It would've been easy to react, to scramble, to force opportunities, to settle for survival. Instead of reacting in panic, we paused in prayer. We fasted. We asked God not just for provision but for precision. Over and over, He came through.

I remember one instance where we were on the brink of a major project launch. Everything seemed to unravel at the last minute: technical delays, financial concerns, and personnel changes. From the outside, it looked like failure was looming. We stopped, gathered our team, and prayed: "God, this is your assignment. Give us your direction." Within forty-eight hours, solutions came from unexpected places: partnerships we didn't see before, favor from a client who accelerated payment, and an internal breakthrough that gave our entire team a renewed sense of unity. That's not a coincidence; that's a covenant.

Proverbs 3:5–6 reminds us, "Trust in the Lord with all your heart and lean not on your own understanding; in all your ways submit to him, and he will make your paths straight." That Scripture isn't just a nice verse for a coffee mug. It's a blueprint for leadership. When you root your work in God, your paths become clearer, even when they're not always easier. You begin to trade striving for surrender. You stop building empires and start advancing Kingdom purpose. Calling God your Chairman means He gets the final say. It means you seek Him not just for blessing but for blueprint. It means you trust Him not just when it's easy, especially when it's not.

PRAYER AS A SECRET WEAPON

Prayer isn't a last resort. It's your first response. It's not just what you do before you act. It's what gives your actions power. It turns ambition into alignment. It transforms effort into effectiveness. Some of my best ideas, clearest breakthroughs, and deepest peace have come not from books or conferences but from moments on my knees. Prayer shifts your perspective, centers your heart, silences fear, and invites God to do what only He can do.

Prayer is not just a religious exercise; it's a spiritual transaction. It's where divine strategies are downloaded. It's where burdens are lifted, and clarity is restored. When you pray, you are not just talking to God. You are surrendering your logic and embracing His leadership. There were times I went into prayer confused and came out clear. Other times, I entered prayer frustrated and came out filled with fresh energy. I've prayed over contracts, deadlines, launches, and disappointments. Time after time, God has shown me that what I thought was an obstacle was actually an opportunity in disguise.

Here are a few ways I've learned to make prayer my power source:

1. Start every day with surrender.

"God, I give You this day, these goals, these conversations." Before the meetings and metrics begin, lay it all before God. He knows what's ahead and wants to lead you into it.

2. Pray Over Your Team

Whether you lead a staff of ten or a crew of two, cover them in wisdom, unity, and clarity. Pray that God gives them strength for their assignments and grace for their growth.

3. Pray Through Your Schedule

Don't assume a meeting on your calendar aligns with God's will. Invite Him into every interaction. Ask Him for discernment, favor, and fruitfulness.

4. End Your Day with Reflection

"Lord, thank You. What did I miss? What should I carry into tomorrow?" Reviewing your day with God creates space for gratitude, correction, and deeper awareness.

5. Pray in the Middle

Don't just pray before and after; pray in real time. Whisper a prayer before the phone call. Take a breath and pray before that difficult conversation. Keep the line open.

Prayer doesn't eliminate work; it multiplies results. It positions you to hear from heaven and act with holy confidence. **Promise + Purpose + Faith + Gratitude = Breakthrough.** Breakthrough doesn't happen solely by grinding hard. It occurs when faith is active, gratitude is practiced, and purpose is clear. Faith believes that even when results are delayed, God is still working.

TRANSFORMING ORDINARY EFFORTS

I've seen this formula transform ordinary efforts into extraordinary outcomes. There were times when the numbers didn't add up, when the strategy wasn't enough, and when motivation was low. As we stayed rooted in God, trusting, thanking, and aligning with His purpose, we saw miracles unfold. Psalm 1:3 paints a picture of this kind of rooted life: "They are like trees planted by streams of water, which yield their fruit in season and whose leaf does not wither; whatever they do prospers." Your discipline becomes fruitful when it is watered by spiritual roots.

STILL WAITING, STILL WALKING

There's something sacred about walking in faith while you're still waiting. Waiting doesn't mean inactivity. It means active trust. It means waking up each day and choosing to believe, even when the results aren't visible and the harvest hasn't arrived. Faith is not proven in the highlight reels of success. It is proven in the quiet, often unseen spaces of endurance. It's in the days when the emails go unanswered, the doors don't open, and the goals remain unmet. In those moments, we find out what we truly believe. Zechariah 4:10 tells us, "Do not despise these small beginnings, for the Lord rejoices to see the work begin." God celebrates the start of your faith walk, empowering you to finish it.

I remember seasons when I was doing all I knew to do: showing up, serving, planning, praying, and still not seeing the results I hoped for. I also remember the peace that would meet me in those moments. A peace that didn't come from metrics, but from abiding in God's presence. The promises of God became my anchor. His voice became my compass. Jennifer and I learned to rejoice in progress, no matter how small. We celebrated faithfulness, not just outcomes. We reminded each other that delay is not denial and that obedience is never wasted.

THE JOURNEY OF BREAKTHROUGH

Here's what I've learned: Breakthrough rarely shows up all at once. It comes in stages, in nudges, and in open doors that once seemed closed. It appears after you've chosen to show up again and again, even when you're tired. If you're still waiting, don't give up. Keep walking, keep sowing, keep praying, and keep praising. The season will shift. The fruit will come. When it does, you'll realize it wasn't just the outcome that mattered; it was who you became while you waited.

That's the beauty of Focused Discipline. It doesn't just help you succeed; it helps you stay rooted. It transforms your waiting season into a growing season and turns what feels like a delay into deep preparation for destiny. When God is your source, you don't have to strive; you abide. In abiding, fruitfulness flows.

SUMMARY: CHAPTER FIFTEEN—KEY TAKEAWAYS

- Focused Discipline is not just about hustle; it is a spiritual posture grounded in your relationship with God.

- Prayer anchors your vision, aligns your heart, and multiplies your efforts. It is your first response, not your last resort.

- God is the ultimate Chairman and CEO. Leading with spiritual sensitivity brings divine insight and direction.

- Daily prayer habits—before, during, and after your work—infuse power and clarity into every action.

- Promise + Purpose + Faith + Gratitude = Breakthrough creates the conditions for supernatural breakthrough. Fruitfulness flows when your roots are deep. Don't rush the harvest; grow through the season.

- Trusting God in the waiting builds spiritual maturity, emotional resilience, and long-term success.

- Root your discipline in something unshakable. When God is the source, your results will carry eternal impact.

CONCLUSION

A LIFE MARKED BY FOCUSED DISCIPLINE

You've made it to the final page; not just of a book, but of a blueprint. Focused Discipline is not just about motivation. It's about transformation. It's about rewiring your habits, refining your mindset, renewing your focus, and ultimately realigning your life with purpose. If you've read this far, it shows you're not just looking for inspiration; you're committed to growth. And that's where everything changes.

Every principle in these chapters, whether about time, habits, mindset, faith, focus, follow-through, or resilience, has one central goal: to help you become the kind of person who finishes well. Not because it's easy. Not because life becomes smoother but because something inside you is anchored in purpose, values, and God.

The world may celebrate talent, speed, or visibility but heaven honors consistency, obedience, and discipline. You don't have to be perfect to make progress. You just need to be intentional. Daily. Quietly. Boldly. Consistently.

So here's my challenge to you: Don't just remember what you've read; live it. Revisit these truths. Reflect on the tools. Recommit to the process. And above all, trust that God will finish what He started in you. This isn't the end. It's the beginning of a more focused, more fruitful, more disciplined life. And you're ready.

Because focused discipline is not just a concept. It's your calling. Now go live it on purpose, with passion, and all the way to the finish—and then keep going beyond what you thought was possible. God bless!!

www.ingramcontent.com/pod-product-compliance
Lightning Source LLC
Chambersburg PA
CBHW070319010526
44107CB00004B/361